Walt Disney's
Snow White and the Seven Dwarfs
An Art in Its Making

Walt Disney's
Snow White and the Seven Dwarfs
An Art in Its Making

featuring
The Collection of Stephen H. Ison

Martin Krause

Linda Witkowski

Indianapolis Museum of Art

New York

First edition

10 9 8 7 6 5 4 3 2 1

Library of Congress Cataloging-in-Publication Data

Krause, Martin F.
    Walt Disney's Snow White and the seven dwarfs : an art in its
making featuring the collection of Stephen H. Ison / Martin Krause,
Linda Witkowski. –– 1st ed.
        p.   cm.
    Includes bibliographical references and index.
    ISBN 0-7868-6144-4
    1. Snow White and the seven dwarfs (Motion picture) 2. Animated
films––Technique. 3. Animated films––United States––History and
criticism. I. Witkowski, Linda A., date.   II. Ison, Stephen H.
III. Title.
PN1997.S6163K73   1994
791.43 ' 72––dc20   94-28121

All works are from the Collection of Stephen H. Ison
Photography by John Geiser, Indianapolis Museum of Art
Edited by Debra Edelstein, Medford, Massachusetts
Designed by JMH Corporation, Indianapolis, Indiana
Production coordinated at the Indianapolis Museum of Art by
 Jane Graham, Publications Manager
Printed at Design Printing Company, Indianapolis, Indiana

Contents

Foreword

Have you ever just once in your life said to yourself, "If there were such things as time machines, I know exactly were I'd go and precisely what I'd do"? My guess is that some "time travelers" would immediately set their coordinates for the previous year's Kentucky Derby, while others might go in search of treasure. I would set my machine for the year 1935, destined for an animation studio on Hyperion Avenue in Hollywood, on an evening when a man named Walt Disney told and acted out the entire story of *Snow White and the Seven Dwarfs* to a group of spellbound young animators. Had I been there for that gathering, I would have witnessed the inception of a piece of animation history that changed forever the way people perceive "cartoons."

Unfortunately, since time machines exist only in the fictional world of H. G. Wells, I've had to settle for a close "second best" to being there through collecting animation art from Disney's *Snow White*. To me every cel, drawing, and watercolor background reproduced in this book represents a special moment "frozen in time."

I've been asked many times over the years why I decided to collect animation art only from *Snow White*. It was never a difficult decision, even in my early collecting days. Though I enjoy and appreciate animation art from other vintage Disney features and shorts, I always liked the idea that *Snow White* was the studio's first animated feature and felt it was a way of paying tribute to a man I had admired since childhood. Here was a person whom I never had the privilege of meeting, yet who touched and influenced my life in many ways. I think people need heroes. Walt Disney was mine.

I also chose to collect *Snow White* for its personal story appeal and artistic style. Though I feel somewhat cheated that I was never able to meet Walt Disney himself, I have had the honor and pleasure of knowing many of the people who worked on the production of *Snow White*. Many of the artisans who greatly influenced the design and feel of the film are artistic treasures in their own right: artists like Joe Grant, Ollie Johnston, Frank Thomas, Marc Davis, Ken O'Connor, Ward Kimball, and Maurice Noble, to name a few. I collect as a tribute to them, as well as for the millions of people who, like me, have been touched by their talents. I don't think I've met anyone who doesn't have an early recollection of the wicked Witch dipping the poisoned apple into the brew or a fond memory of the antics and personalities of the seven dwarfs.

I often go into the special gallery I had constructed for displaying my *Snow White* collection just to admire the results of so much talent focused on what has become such an important piece of American history. As I walk from frame to frame, I sometimes feel that I don't *really* own this collection, but am instead merely its steward. What started out as a hobby has become so much more than I ever dreamed. I've come, at last, to understand what other serious collectors before me have learned: As a collector, you have an obligation to preserve what you have been fortunate enough to amass. You must realize that, if you do your job well, the art will outlive you. So you must educate yourself on how to protect your treasures for future generations. In a sense, then, you're only borrowing the art for a while in hopes that someday someone will take up where you left off.

With that in mind, I guess there *is* another place I would go if I could travel through time. I would program my machine for the year 2037 to celebrate the 100th anniversary of the premiere of *Snow White and the Seven Dwarfs* and to see if the first Disney feature is still "the fairest one of all." My belief is that it will be, and my hope is that the collection I have painstakingly put together will have been joined with many other great pieces (or collections) of vintage Disney art in a permanent exhibition constructed for succeeding admirers. What better way to honor the hundreds of men and women who spent countless hours sketching at animation tables, exhaustively developing the characters and stories that we have come to know and love, and to recognize the many other areas involved in the creative process called animation. Each piece, a work of art; each one a moment frozen in time.

Stephen Ison

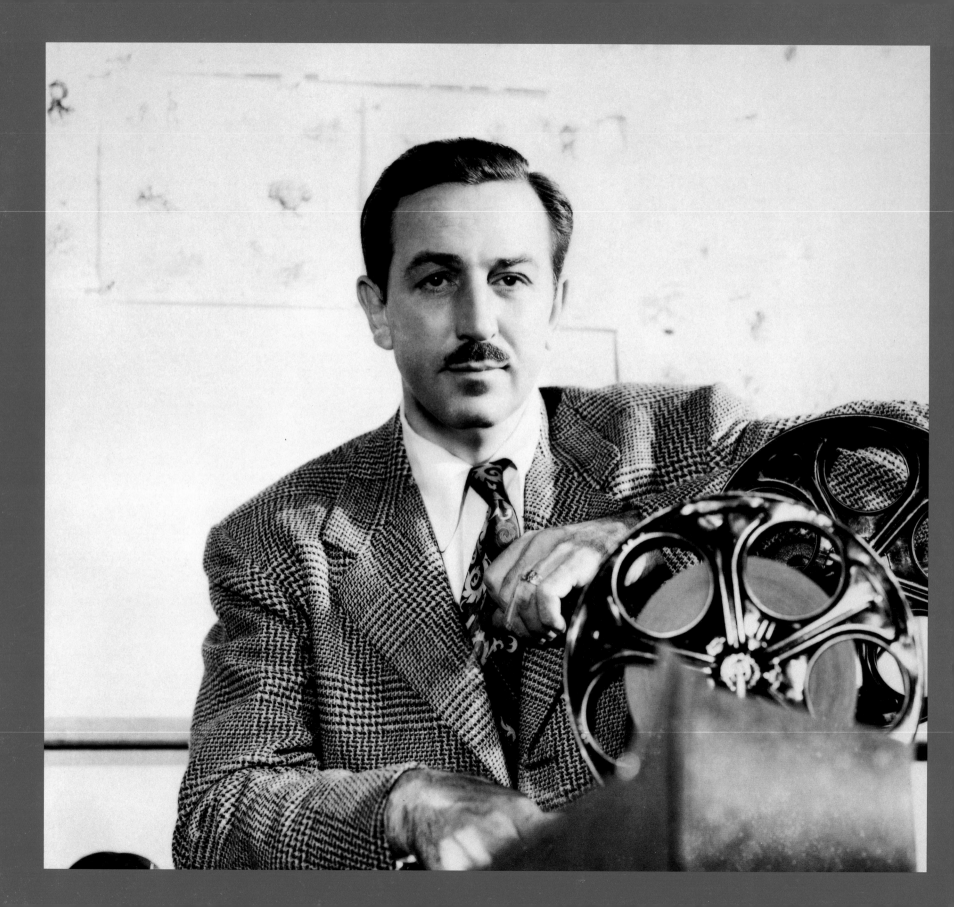

The Creative Art of
Snow White and the Seven Dwarfs

Overture

Most people go to "movies"; some go to "films." Most would describe movies as popular entertainment and films as more artistic; but they would be distinguishing between things that are technically the same and only subjectively different. Both movies and films depend on a length of celluloid containing thousands of transparent still pictures passing through the projector at a rate of twenty-four frames per second, fast enough to make each separate frame imperceptible. Both are truly motion pictures, and animation is the ultimate form. It does not break down live action into frames, but builds the illusion of motion, picture by picture, frame by frame.

Whether animation should be considered a legitimate art was a question that Walt Disney preferred to leave to the "professors."[1] The debate as to whether its forebear, photography, can ascend to artistry has gone on for the 150 years since its invention. Whether its descendants—movies, television, and video—need apply is an even more open question. When sixty years ago Walt Disney embarked on the making of Snow White and the Seven Dwarfs, he was not making an art film, but rather the world's first animated feature. For the fledgling Walt Disney Studios to survive, it had to prove popular. It was made for entertainment, but it was at the same time a monumental artistic endeavor.

In spite of Disney's intentions and regardless of where the debate is today, many of America's art critics felt that Disney had already transformed the humble cartoon into a new art form even before he began Snow White in 1934. Early the previous year the widely published art critic for the Philadelphia Inquirer, Dorothy Grafly, had enthused:

> Walt Disney has at last given the world what should have come through established art channels— the creative exploit of the animated cartoon in color, probably the first genuinely American art since that of the indigenous Indian.[2]

At the same time the exhibition The Art of Mickey Mouse was beginning the circuit of art museums, traveling from The Philadelphia Art Alliance to the Milwaukee Art Institute to the Toledo Museum of Art. And at the same time the editor of The Art News was predicting an exciting future for the animated film:

> The cinema, with its wealth of pictorial possibilities, appears to have reached a point in its development when a new art form of special significance may be said to have received its inception. The animated cartoon, that inventive though humble agent of the screen which brought Mickey Mouse and his host of cut-up cousins into such world-wide acclaim, has taken on new life with the advent of color, and the past few weeks have seen the first of a new series of these features all aglow with rainbow hues that argue endless delights to come. . . . It is not difficult to imagine the screen made thrilling with scenes from Moby Dick drawn and colored by Rockwell Kent and worked out as to detail by the various technicians such as Mr. Disney has at his command. Then think of Alice in Wonderland with all the Teniel fixings coming into new life on the screen, or any of a host of pictorial characters that have rested so far on the printed page. . . . Romance, adventure, poetic flights of highest fancy, all at the bidding of our new screen geniuses, will doubtless course over the screens of the future with musical accompaniments by the best composers. The possibilities are indeed endless and the vistas thus opened up alluring to say the least. Mr. Disney has started a new art that is destined to go a long way.[3]

The journal rightfully called it "A New Art in the Making." The challenge to Disney was how to fulfill this prediction. He succeeded with his Snow White and the Seven Dwarfs, which would be four years in its making.

Walt Disney

Opening Credits

1933

In January 1933, as the art editors pondered Walt Disney's future, he was doing the same. Though he had turned just thirty-one the previous month, he had already been in the cartoon business for thirteen years, ten of them on his own. He had his own studio in Los Angeles, and from its expanding offices his growing corps of storymen, layout men, animators, assistant animators, inkers, painters, cameramen, and musicians were turning out "shorts." These seven-minute, action-packed, gag-filled cartoons, released at a rate of more than one a month, were preceding the live-action features in movie houses across America. Disney was a household name and at the top of his game. But the present was not entirely rosy and animation's horizon, which *The Art News* placed in his hands, was broader than anyone except Disney could realistically imagine.

Disney was not a pioneering animator. That credit fell to the likes of Winsor McKay, who had brought *Gertie the Trained Dinosaur* to the vaudeville screen in 1909; Max Fleischer, the inventor of *Ko-Ko the Clown*; and Pat Sullivan, with his *Felix the Cat*. In fact, Disney was never better than a marginally trained and indifferent cartoonist.

Yet he was smart enough to admit it and therefore entrusted the work that bore his name to others, beginning with Ub Iwerks in the early years.

But Disney did know animation from the bottom up. He found his first job in animation in 1920 with Kansas City Film Ad. His first task was basic stop-action commercial animation. Cut-out paper puppets with moveable joints were pinned to a board. Moving the arms and legs and photographing each adjustment created a rough illusion of motion. Disney rapidly progressed to drawn animation, in which a sequence of drawings replaced the articulated cut-outs.

From there he moved to cel animation, which was the industry standard for the New York-based cartoonists whose films were entertaining the populace in America's movie theaters. Instead of paper, cel animation uses transparent sheets of cellulose nitrate ("cels") as the drawing surface. These sheets are placed individually atop a drawn or painted background and photographed sequentially; when projected at the era's standard speed of sixteen frames per second, the character seemed to act in a landscape.

In 1923 Disney, his brother Roy (a former bank teller), and Iwerks struck out for Los Angeles. There they produced a series of shorts, based nominally on

Alice in Wonderland, that combined animation with live action. By 1926 they were successful enough to open the Walt Disney Studio on Hyperion Avenue, with a production team of six.[4]

The next year Disney introduced the character Oswald the Lucky Rabbit in *Poor Papa*, his first fully animated short. The Oswald series was distributed by Universal Pictures, which obtained the rights for $2,250 per cartoon and a contract for a new release to appear every two weeks. Oswald was a quick success. When the contract was up in early 1928, Disney asked for an increase of $250 per cartoon. Instead, Universal offered $450 less.[5] Disney could not afford to say yes; Universal took Oswald.

Disney replaced him with an even more enduring character, Mickey Mouse. The first two Mickey shorts, *Plane Crazy* and *The Gallopin' Gaucho*, did not find a buyer, but the third, *Steamboat Willie*, was a sensation. The audience at New York's Colony Theater on November 18, 1928, saw the birth of this international screen icon, given his shape by Iwerks and his voice by Walt Disney. *Steamboat Willie* was one of the first viable films of any kind with the sound synchronized on the film rather than on a separately recorded

Production background for Snow White, *1937*

phonographic disc, the way in which Al Jolson, in *The Jazz Singer*, had broken the sound barrier of filmdom only thirteen months earlier.

Now the big studios wanted Disney, but they wanted Mickey Mouse even more. Disney declined. After Oswald, he had learned the virtue, if not the financial benefits, of independence.

The theater managers cried for "more mice," and Disney complied with a steady stream of fifteen in the next two years. As an independent producer, he could also offer them something they did not want, the first of his Silly Symphonies, *The Skeleton Dance*. The advent of sound had inspired Disney and his animators to create this new and unfamiliar aural-visual experience. While *Steamboat Willie* had featured the gag of Minnie Mouse cranking a goat's tail like a Victrola to produce the strains of the homey *Turkey in the Straw*, the first Silly Symphony animated a venerable Dance of Death to selections of classical music, including Saint-Saëns *Danse Macabre*. The theater managers were not buying, so Disney arranged his own booking at Los Angeles's Carthay Circle Theatre in May 1929. The positive critical response ensured that the Silly Symphonies were well launched. Then, in October, the stock market crashed.

Even if Disney, and the film industry in general, benefited while others lost during the ensuing years of the Great Depression—movies being cheap entertainment that offered a respite in hard times—

the studio could not avoid the economic jitters. But the probability of scarce funds had always been an accepted fact of life for what was now Walt Disney Productions. While Disney's advance per cartoon had grown from $2,250 from Universal in 1927 to $7,000 from Columbia Pictures in 1930 to $15,000 from United Artists in 1932, there never was much profit.[6] Hollywood sources said that Disney took "two and seven-eighths cents out of every three he got and put it back into studio experiments."[7]

First there were the initial studio expenses in 1926, then, in 1928, the scarce and therefore expensive sound equipment. Furthermore, with the advent of sound, the engineers at Western Electric concluded that the traditional standard of cranking a camera sixteen revolutions a second was inconsistent with the speed of movie projectors, which they found to run between twenty and twenty-six frames per second. They averaged it to twenty-four frames per second, which became the new standard.[8] For makers of live-action pictures this simply meant additional film, but for Disney it meant an increase of nearly 25 percent in the number of drawings needed for the same length of film. Not only were sound men and musicians added to the payroll to make use of the new equipment, but also more animators. Ben Sharpsteen, Dick Huemer, Dave Hand, Norm Ferguson, and Jack King, veterans of the New York cartoon studios, were recruited. All contributed by 1930 to the higher quality and complexity of each short and the corresponding reduction by about half in the quantity from the

Animation drawing for Steamboat Willie, 1928

HE SLACKS UP AND VINE SPRINGS AWAY FROM POST

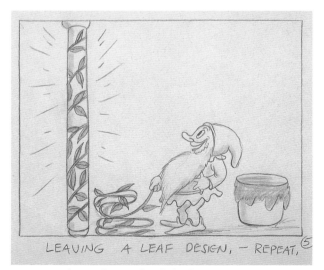

LEAVING A LEAF DESIGN, — REPEAT,

Sequence of an early gag sketch for the "Bed-Building Sequence" in Snow White

two-a-month rate of 1926. To accommodate this growth, a sound stage and animation building were added to the Hyperion lot in 1930 and 1931, respectively.

All of this cost more than the rentals of the shorts could cover, but Disney was not one to let money stand in the way of a good idea. He left this financial challenge to his brother Roy, who would be dubbed in Disneyese the only living "mathemagician" of "artonomics."[9] He established Walt Disney Enterprises in 1929 to cash in on the craze for Mickey Mouse. Licenses for watches, toys, handkerchiefs, and sundry other spin-off products bearing Mickey's image were granted to companies across the country, and the generated royalties funded the expansion. Roy also negotiated the more advantageous contract for the shorts with United Artists at the beginning of 1932, which his brother more than spent on a newly perfected technology—color.

Although attempts to join color and film dated to the turn of the century, the process was still experimental thirty years later.[10] Then in 1932 Herbert Kalmus perfected his three-strip Technicolor process, in which a specifically designed camera fitted with rotating filters broke down a color image into red, blue, and green negatives that, when processed, reproduced a positive full-color print. This new technology was not yet applicable to live-action motion pictures, but it was useable in animation. Disney cornered the market by entering into a two-year, exclusive-use contract for Technicolor. His current Silly Symphony, *Flowers and Trees*, animated to the music of

Mendelssohn, Rossini, Schubert, and Chopin, was already in production as a black-and-white short. Disney had the cels re-inked and repainted in colors and the backgrounds redone in watercolor; it was released in July 1932. In November it won for Disney his first Academy Award, and the first given to an animated cartoon.

Mickey Mouse continued to be the popular favorite; the Silly Symphonies were the critical darlings, particularly after *Flowers and Trees*. The first Silly Symphonies in color led Dorothy Grafly to conclude:

The Mickey Mouse films are the last word in the animated comic strip; the Silly Symphonies are the triumph of a new art. In these, with the brush stroke of his imagination, Walt Disney paints a sequence of movements and resulting emotional episodes that do for art what the orchestra does for music. They make possible not one scene as on canvas, but the interrelation of many scenes that together produce a new emotional experience. The Silly Symphonies are thus unique in the world of our day. . . . The Silly Symphony, at its best, is a consistent rhythmic flow of sound, form, and color that bears its audience away from the physical into a world of creative enchantment.[11]

Walt Disney, too, saw the Silly Symphonies as a personal progression:

> I knew the diversifying of the business would be the salvation of it. I tried that in the beginning, because I didn't want to be stuck with the Mouse. So I went into the Silly Symphonies. It did work out. The Symphonies led to the features; without the work I did on the Symphonies, I'd never have been prepared to even tackle *Snow White*.[12]

Disney recognized that Mickey Mouse, being an improvement on the established form of cartoon, could survive without the new technology. He remained in black and white until 1935, when he entered the colorful world of the Silly Symphonies in *The Band Concert*. During that time the Mickey Mouse shorts continued to be the province of Disney's long-time animators and his New York recruits, who had been grounded in and excelled in burlesque action.

The Silly Symphonies, however, were the training ground for a new crop of artists coming to Disney directly from art schools. In more opportune financial times they might have opted for jobs as illustrators of books or magazines, but during the Depression, the publishers were not hiring; Disney was. These artists knew a lot about drawing but nothing of the far different demands of animation; the old hands knew little but. For the benefit of both groups, Disney engaged Don Graham of the Chouinard School of Art in Los Angeles to teach night classes at the studio, and the first

Cel setup for King Neptune, *Disney's second Technicolor Silly Symphony, 1932*

meeting of his Disney Art School was held on November 15, 1932.[13]

At the turning of the year 1933, the editors of *The Art News,* excited by the potential they had just seen in the two inaugural Technicolor Silly Symphonies, *Flowers and Trees* and *King Neptune,* found Disney uniquely positioned to take animation another step further. They saw him becoming a storyteller, borrowing from the realm of books—perhaps Herman Melville's *Moby Dick* or Lewis Carroll's *Alice in Wonderland*—and making animate what to that date had rested inanimate on the printed page. Implicitly, they were proposing subjects that could not be treated as short subjects and stories that took longer to tell. These were untested waters.

The critics' confidence in Disney was no greater than his own. The idea of bringing to life the illustrated fairy tale had first been broached to him in 1930 by employee Jack Cutting, who laid before Disney some of his favorite books, illustrated by the American N. C. Wyeth and the Englishman Arthur Rackham:

I said, "Walt, wouldn't it be wonderful if we could make animation like these books?" I remember he looked them over—he may not have been clever at talking about it, but he had innate sensitivity—and he said that it would be difficult, and then he said, "Maybe. Someday."[14]

"Someday" might have come as early as the next year, when he contemplated a film based on *Alice in Wonderland,* only to be beaten to the draw by Commonwealth Pictures Corporation, which released a live-action version. Or it might have been a year or two later, when he discussed the same story as a feature-length production with Mary Pickford as a live Alice in a cartoon wonderland. His plans were again preempted, this time by Paramount's Cary Grant, W. C. Fields, Gary Cooper vehicle in 1933.[15] But by mid-1933 the last pieces of the puzzle leading to his first animated feature-length film fell into place.

Disney conceived his first full-length animated venture as a "Feature Symphony,"[16] and saw the Symphonies as its testing ground, so it was crucial for him to gauge the popular appeal of a Silly Symphony with a tight story line, original music, and memorable characters. Disney introduced this formula in *Three Little Pigs,* his thirty-sixth Silly Symphony, released on May 27, 1933. He could not have been more pleased with the product and the public's response.

Disney and his team took the elements of an old English fable and retold it in the American vernacular. They simplified the story into a compact little melodrama in which the vice of laziness, personified by two of the little pigs, is punished with a huff and a puff by the very big and very bad wolf, while the virtue of industriousness, in the guise of the third brother pig, triumphs over evil. These personalities were animated by Dick Lundy and Fred Moore (the pigs) and by Norm

Ferguson (the wolf), and the whole story was tied together by the refrain "Who's Afraid of the Big Bad Wolf?," written by Disney's in-house composer, Frank Churchill.

Three Little Pigs proved even more popular than Mickey Mouse and was reportedly "the most popular film ever made" to that date.[17] "Who's Afraid of the Big Bad Wolf?" became the studio's first hit song, and the film garnered the Academy Award for Short Subject-Cartoons in 1933.[18]

Disney now had a formula for a feature. He had the technological edge in sound and color. He had on staff a hit songwriter. And by the end of the year he had the human resources at hand, with 12 story- and gagmen, 40 animators, 45 assistant animators, 30 inkers and painters, a 24-piece orchestra, and 26 other technical and support staff members.[19] More were coming, attracted by the innovative *Three Little Pigs.*[20] Based on his faultless track record, he was given a long line of credit by the Bank of America. The current thought at the studio was that a feature would be the equivalent of a string of twelve seven-minute shorts,[21] at $20,000 each, so Disney set the initial budget at $250,000.[22] In reality it would take more staff, more time, and more money, and the feature would become much, much more than anyone could have imagined in late 1933, when, by Disney's own account, the idea of making *Snow White* the world's first animated full-length feature film began to crystallize in his mind.[23]

The Story
1934

At the outset Disney recognized the importance of choosing a subject for his feature that was "known and beloved in practically every country in the world."[24] He immediately locked onto the genre of fable, myth, and fairy tale, and from the list of Silly Symphonies released in the wake of *Three Little Pigs* comes an indication of the sorts of subjects he was looking at over the next year: *Old King Cole* (released July 29, 1933), *The Pied Piper* (September 16), *The Night Before Christmas* (December 9), *Grasshopper and the Ants* (February 10, 1934), and *The Wise Little Hen* (June 6). The brevity of a Mother Goose story or an Aesop's fable precluded their consideration for a feature, but two longer tales, *Jack and the Beanstalk* and *Gulliver's Travels,* were retailored as Mickey Mouse shorts in the same span: *Giantland* (November 25, 1933) and *Gulliver Mickey* (May 19, 1934).

Disney had already considered *Alice in Wonderland,* and, after *Three Little Pigs*, he discussed *Babes in Toyland* with RKO Pictures, which owned the rights.[25] Perhaps at this early date he began thinking of *The Wizard of Oz*, which was then a Samuel Goldwyn property.[26] Given Disney's decision that his "Feature Symphony" would have a major musical component, these two

properties were natural candidates. Victor Herbert's *Babes in Toyland* had been written as an operetta and had toured for years after its Broadway premiere in 1903. L. Frank Baum's *The Wonderful Wizard of Oz* had been dramatized and set to music at the time it was published in 1900. These discussions came to naught, and Metro-Goldwyn-Mayer would release both, with Laurel and Hardy starring in the 1934 *Babes in Toyland* and Judy Garland in the 1939 *The Wizard of Oz.*

The Grimm brothers' tale *Snow White* had also been dramatized for the stage in 1912, with Marguerite Clark in the lead role. Disney remembered having seen the "play" with money he saved from his newspaper route, but it was not the stage play that he saw in Kansas City—it ran for only seventy-two matinee performances on Broadway[27]—but rather its 1916 silent-film restaging with Marguerite Clark reprising her role. Later Disney would cite this vivid memory as the sentimental reason behind his choice of *Snow White* for his first feature,[28] but practicality weighed heavily as well:

The seven dwarfs, we knew, were "naturals" for the medium of our pictures. In them we could instill boundless humor, not only as to their physical appearances, but in their mannerisms, personalities, voices, and actions. In addition,

with most of the action taking place in and around the dwarfs' cottage in the woods, we realized that there was great opportunity for introducing appealing little birds and animals of the type we've had success with in the past. Lastly, the human characters were fanciful enough to allow us a great deal of leeway in our treatment of them.[29]

The "we" suggests that the decision was somehow mutually made, but it rested solely with Disney. He first shared his decision with his senior personnel in the summer of 1934, and almost secretly set a few select storymen and a couple of top artists to work in a room next to his office.

In the most familiar version of Jacob and Wilhelm Grimm's ten-page tale, Snow White is born a princess, but her mother, the Queen, dies in childbirth. The new Queen, her stepmother, is proud, vain, and, as her magic looking-glass compliments her, of unsurpassed beauty. When Snow White reaches seven years, however, the glass reveals that the girl is now "the fairest one of all." Filled with envy and hate, the Queen instructs her huntsman to take her stepdaughter into the woods, kill her, and bring back her heart. The huntsman proves incapable of the deed and leaves Snow White to run away into

Atmosphere watercolor of the Queen's laboratory for Snow White *by background painter Maurice Noble*

the forest. At evening she comes upon the dwarfs' cottage and falls asleep. The seven dwarfs return from their work underground, discover the stranger, and decide to let her stay if she will keep house for them. The Queen, apprised by the magic mirror of the huntsman's treachery and of the whereabouts of Snow White, adopts the disguise of an old peddler woman and tries three times to kill her stepdaughter, first by suffocation, then by poisoned hair comb, and finally by poisoned apple. One bite leaves Snow White in a deathlike sleep. The dwarfs, having successfully revived the girl from the earlier attempts, now think her dead. They are, however, incapable of burying her, so they fabricate a glass coffin, over which they and the forest animals keep vigil. Long after, a prince comes upon the coffin. Enraptured by the beauty of the girl, he asks and receives the dwarfs' permission to bear away the coffin. While doing so he stumbles and the piece of apple flies from her throat. Snow White awakens and agrees to marry the Prince. The evil Queen is invited to their feast. When she recognizes Snow White, whom she had thought long dead, she flies into a rage and dances to her death in red-hot iron shoes that Snow White had had fashioned to exact her revenge.

The story's characters and its plot were so familiar worldwide that Disney had to respect them. But to make the story into a film would require not only its retelling in the newly pictured language of contemporary movie-making, but also a restaging in a make-believe environment with inventive characters to whom the

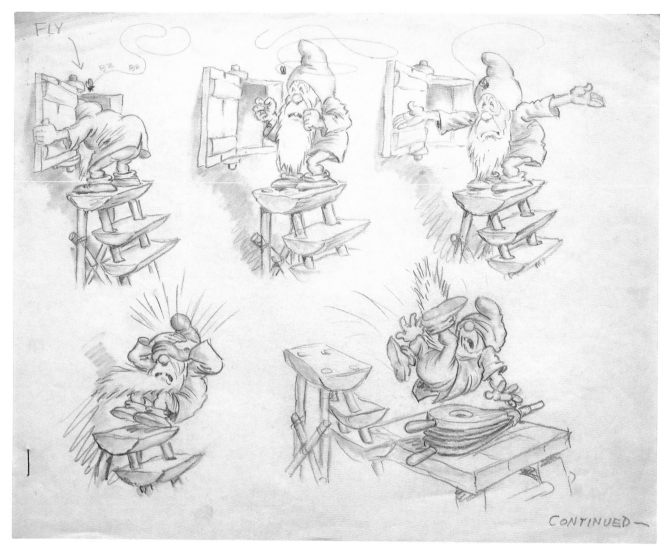

Early gag sketches for the dwarfs by storyman Earl Hurd, 1934

EARL

Disney animators, and through them the audience, could relate. For this imaginary world "there was no geography."[30]

The initial platting of Snow White's world was entrusted to a few of Disney's storymen. Many of them were former animators who had been recruited out of New York, but who were being phased out by Disney when *Snow White* began. He moved them into the Story Department.[31] In this group were Dave Hand, Webb Smith, Harry Reeves, and Ted Sears. It was not a demotion, for as Disney wrote in a memo to Sears, "I honestly feel that the heart of our organization is the Story Department. We must have good stories."[32]

In their new positions they influenced the first story outlines for *Snow White*. From the perspective of a new animator, Frank Thomas, these men represented the old school:

> Disney started with animators who were all entertainers—comic strip men, newspaper cartoonists— people like that. And the big thing to them was the gag, and that was big to Walt with the cartoons during the twenties. . . . At the start [of *Snow White*] everything was gags, gags, gags and now Walt was seeing something new and more things that he could do with animation, and the layout men would give him new drawings, and everybody was coming up with new ideas and so Walt was going "What have I got here?" He was like an organist playing all the stops.[33]

By August 9, 1934, the first outline of the picture was consigned to paper. Thereafter, the story meetings were recorded by a staff stenographer and circulated to involved parties.

At the outset, it was felt that the seven dwarfs would carry the film. They were, as Disney said, "naturals" for the gagmen. The dwarfs were to be given seven distinct personalities and were to be named (unlike the anonymous seven in most versions of Grimm) for their leading personality traits. A list of fifty possibilities was drawn up, including Hoppy, Awful, Weepy, Gabby, Gloomy, and Flabby. Those six did not make the cut, but Happy, Sleepy, Sneezy, Grumpy, and Bashful did. By October 9 the first tentative group of seven had been named and given some idiosyncrasies: the ever-lagging Wheezy, the excitable Jumpy, the bashful, floppy-eared Baldy [or Bashful], the deaf and crabby Grumpy, the jovial and laughing Happy, the pompous leader Doc, and the ever-dozing Sleepy.[34]

On October 22 a new tentative "cast of characters" was listed, and many in the cast were given recognizable equivalents from motion pictures or radio:

Snow White:
Janet Gaynor type—14 years old.
The Prince:
Douglas Fairbanks type—18 years old.
The Queen:
A mixture of Lady Macbeth and the Big Bad Wolf—Her beauty is sinister, mature, plenty of curves—She becomes ugly and menacing when scheming and mixing her poisons—Magic fluids transform her into an old witchlike hag—her dialogue and action are over-melodramatic, verging on the ridiculous.
The Huntsman:
A minor character—Big and tough—40 years old—The Queen's trusted henchman. But hasn't the heart to murder an innocent girl.
The Seven Dwarfs:
Happy:
A glad boy—Sentimental—Addicted to happy proverbs—His jaw slips out of its socket when he talks, thus producing a goofy speech mannerism.
Sleepy:
Sterling Holloway—Always going to sleep—Always swatting at a fly on the end of his nose.
Doc:
The leader and spokesman of the Dwarfs—Pompous, wordy, great dignity—Feels his superiority, but is more or less a windbag.
Bashful:
Has a high peaked skull which makes him ashamed to take off his hat—blushing, hesitating, squirmy, giggly.

Jumpy:
Joe Twerp—Like a chap in constant fear of being goosed—Nervous, excited—His words and sentences mixed up.
Grumpy:
Typical dyspeptic and grouch—Pessimist—Woman-hater—The last to make friends with Snow White.
Seventh:
Deaf, always listening intently—Happy—Quick movements—Spry.
Prince's Horse:
This gallant white charger understands but cannot talk—Like Tom Mix's horse Tony—the Prince's pal.
Magic Mirror:
The Queen's unwilling slave—Its masklike face appears when invoked—It speaks in a weird voice.[35]

The same outline contained a fairly lengthy synopsis of the story, divided into acts and beginning with the device of "the story book opening":

We see a book bearing on its cover the title and author, the Brothers Grimm. It opens to the credit page. Then, as its beautifully illuminated pages turn, we read the prologue which plants the Queen as a vain and murderous witch; Snow White as a mistreated victim of the Queen's jealousy and greed for power, the Magic Mirror, and the reason for the Prince's visit to the palace. In short, the story book opening is a footage-saving device that carries us well into the plot and interesting action, and also establishes the situation and characters in advance.

Rather than spend too much of our energy at the present time in working out the first and less important sequences, Walt prefers to start actual work at the point where Snow White finds the cottage of the Seven Dwarfs. FROM THIS POINT ON, our basic plot development is fairly definitely established. What happens UP TO THAT TIME is still rather hazy.[36]

It became somewhat clearer on November 6, when a new synopsis outlined and plotted the story much as it would be committed to film (Appendix A).

After three months of editing, the story is much changed from that recorded by the Grimm brothers. The episodes of Snow White's birth, her mother's death, and the evil Queen's dance of death have been deleted. The first attempt on Snow White's life by suffocation with bodice laces is also gone. The Queen no longer disguises herself as an apple peddler but effects a transformation into a hag in her laboratory. Snow White is no longer awakened by the dislodging from her throat of the poisoned apple, but rather by the more romantic kiss, borrowed from another of the Grimms' fairy tales, *The Sleeping Beauty*.[37] The Prince has an expanded role, as do the dwarfs and the forest animals. Songs have been added and placed at appropriate intervals. The whole story is retold in eighteen paragraphs, each comprising an act or a "sequence" as it was known at Disney, which describe in cinematic format episodes of romance, adventure and drama relieved by sequences of comedy.

Work was to begin, the synopsis concluded, on the broadly caricatured dwarfs and personable animals, who were cartoon types that the Disney staff had perfected in the short subjects:

> For the time being, we will concentrate entirely upon scenes in which only Snow White, the Dwarfs, and their bird and animal friends appear. . . . Please sketch up your ideas ready to submit by Tuesday November Thirteenth, 1934. Running Gags! Character Building Gags! Action and Dialogue Gags for quick laughs![38]

The untried human characters—the pretty Snow White, the handsome Prince, and the beautiful Queen— would prove much more difficult to render believably. To test his animators' potential for the princess, Disney had prepared a new Silly Symphony, *The Goddess of Spring*, based on a Greek myth and centered on the delicate goddess Persephone and her abduction to the underworld. Released on November 3, 1934, its unconvincing animation proved that the current crop of animators were not masters of this task. Innovative work would be required.

Disney summed up the status of the project as it stood at the end of the year:

> 1934 found us with a pretty complete adaptation of the story, and thousands of sketches, gags, backgrounds, character models and so on had been worked out. Because we had no precedent for this undertaking, we had to discard much of the preliminary material—material which had meant hours of hard work.[39]

Much of what had been worked out in story research and character development *would* appear on screen, but not for three years. The time between December 1934 and the premiere on December 21, 1937, was spent in the laborious process of storyboarding, scripting, orchestrating, visualizing, and animating the story. Not less time consuming was the film's realignment to Disney's constantly maturing thinking and his corresponding insistence that the staff upgrade itself or be upgraded to his ever-higher expectations.

Sequence

The head animation duties in 1935 were in the hands of Ham Luske, Les Clark, and Fred Moore, who had had no training other than what Disney had offered them through Don Graham's night classes and through constant work. Norm Ferguson, who had proven himself more malleable to the evolving Disney style in his work on the Big Bad Wolf than had his New York confreres, was not kicked upstairs to the Story Department. He also commanded as large a salary as Disney, $300 a week.[40] These artists would tutor the next generation of Disney animators.

Disney anticipated the need for new and more skilled artists for the feature. Allowing for a period of incubation within his system, he instructed Don Graham, who headed the now full-time Disney Art School: "I need three hundred artists—find them."[41]

Graham first culled the list of his students at Chouinard, beginning with Frank Thomas, who came to Disney in the summer of 1934, and Ollie Johnston, who was hired on January 28, 1935. At about the same time a group of former Stanford students arrived—Jim Algar, Thor Putnam, and Jack Boyd—along with Milt Kahl, who had also studied in the Bay area.[42] There was a contingent from Santa Barbara, including Ward Kimball, hired in April 1934, and Sam Armstrong, who would head the Background Department. Kendall O'Connor and Marc Davis, both former students at the California School of Fine Arts in San Francisco, arrived in 1935, in response to the classified ads that Graham had placed. Most of these new arrivals would contribute enough to *Snow White and the Seven Dwarfs* in the next three years to be included by Disney among the select seventy-five receiving screen credit for the film, but at the time they were hired the feature was hardly more than a rumor to them.[43] The new men were cast into the studio's so-called bullpen, where, for $15 a week,[44] twenty-five to thirty artists at a time began to learn the animation process by "inbetweening."

Inbetweeners were the animators of the lowest rank. They were assigned to draw the interludes between the important points of a character's action that had been roughed out by the head animator and cleaned up by his assistant.

All the artists, new and old, were strongly encouraged to attend, both on Walt's time and on their own, the various classes that Don Graham held from eight in the morning until nine at night. Instruction stressed line drawing over color, and in life classes the artists drew from the live model and from animals brought onto the lot. There were regular trips to the zoo at Griffith Park down the street from the studio and twice-weekly action-analysis classes, in which short pieces of live-action film were studied to learn the fundamentals of motion. Some of the artists missed the point of this exercise, as noted by Disney in a 1935 memo to Graham:

> A good many of the men
> misinterpret the idea of studying
> the actual motion. They think it is
> our purpose merely to duplicate
> these things. This misconception
> should be cleared up for all.
> I definitely feel that we cannot
> do the fantastic things based
> on the real, unless we first
> know the real.[45]

The purpose of all the classes was not to turn the studio artists into imitators of nature, which had little practical application on the job, but rather to make them such intuitive observers of nature that they could caricature it, which was the heart of the business. As Frank Thomas remembers:

> Walt always told us that the most
> important thing you have to do is
> observe. Observe. Watch dogs.
> Watch people. Watch different
> kinds of people. Watch what they
> wear. Watch what they do.

*Preliminary background of the dwarfs'
bedroom by Maurice Noble*

Cel setup for
Woodland Cafe, *1937*

See what things show their personalities; which things reveal their thought processes.[46]

But the most important instruction received by the young artists came through their working proximity to more experienced men. "I've been to Graham's art school a lot," Les Clark revealed, "but I've learned more from the fellows working with me here at the studio than I ever did in an art class."[47]

If the beginning artist survived the capriciousness of George Drake's supervision of the inbetweeners, his advancement could be rapid. The head animators were taking on assistants to work on the shorts and to prepare for their anticipated work on the feature. Ward Kimball for instance, twenty years old upon his arrival at Disney in 1934, began as an inbetweener on the Silly Symphony *The Wise Little Hen*. By the end of the year he had been taken on by Ham Luske as an assistant to work on *The Tortoise and the Hare*. Two years later he advanced to independent animation on *Woodland Cafe* (released on March 13, 1937). He then moved on to the feature.[48] Just ten months after hiring on, Frank Thomas became Fred Moore's assistant to help finish up *Mickey's Kangaroo* (released April 13, 1935). Thomas, who admits that at the time he could not distinguish a good animation drawing from a bad one, remembers the advice Moore gave him:

I'm going to explain [what makes a good animation drawing] to you around 460 times, and each time you're going to say, "Yeah, I know, you told me that before." And you're going to be sure that you understand it. But you won't. And so, don't worry about it. Just keep drawing and listening, and all of a sudden, one day, somewhere around 460, a light will go on and you'll say, "Oh, that's what you meant all along!" And he was right, I did.[49]

Thomas worked with Moore on shorts for almost one year, after which he was promoted to animate on his own beginning with *Mickey's Circus*. Oliie Johnston replaced him as Moore's assistant on March 23, 1936.[50]

In anticipation of the feature, "the whole studio grew like Topsy; apartment houses were leased all over the neighborhood."[51] The Animation Department was expanding. The Annex was built across Hyperion Avenue to house the inbetweeners, the Paint Lab, Graham's school, and the Ink and Paint Department.[52] For these departments full-scale work on the feature was still a year or two away. At the beginning of 1935 *Snow White and the Seven Dwarfs* remained the project of a handful of individuals working out of the office next to Disney's. The first substantive information that most of the studio received was in a mass meeting at mid-year, during which Disney gave them a full-blown rendition. As Disney veteran Ken Anderson, recalled:

We went to the sound stage where there was a tier of seats and Walt told us the story of *Snow White*. It started about 7:30 and went on

Preliminary backgrounds of the dwarfs' cottage by Maurice Noble

till 11. We were spellbound. The lights were all on and they were on us, not him. He was all by himself and he acted out this fantastic story. He would *become* the Queen. He would *become* the dwarfs. He was an incredible actor, a born mime.[53] When he got to the end he told us that that was going to be our first feature. It was a shock to all of us because we knew how hard it was to do a cartoon short.[54]

Disney did not "read" the story that the Grimm brothers had committed to paper in 1812 but retold it in his own words. While the premise for the feature belonged to the brothers Grimm, the film would belong to Disney.

When the story research had been completed and the characters tentatively identified as they had been at the end of 1934, the "look" of the story and of its cast had to be set and story sketches begun. The studio was not departmentalized in those days, and anybody with an idea, a gag, or an inspiration about what a character might look like or do was encouraged to submit it. Bonuses were offered from the outset to encourage such thinking.[55] But the process of stylizing the film—its settings, its architecture, its props, and the first manifestations of the principal characters—was generally in the hands of Albert Hurter.

Hurter had come to the studio in 1932 from New York with a background in newspaper cartooning. He started as an animator but was soon unleashed to employ his imagination in

conceptualizing a few Silly Symphonies and then *Snow White*. "Albert was one of the few intellectuals around the studio who would have been familiar with all of the art movements of the past," remembers Joe Grant, who began collaborating with Hurter in mid-1935. "He was a little bit shy of the modern movement, but he was very open-minded and extraordinarily talented."[56] Their shared duty on *Snow White* was to create its "atmosphere" and to provide inspirational drawings for use by the Story Department, the Layout Department, and the animators. For their own inspiration they turned to a wealth of illustrated books. "We tapped the world for material," says Grant.[57]

Given the European origins of the story, European sources were of most use. Arthur Rackham (1867–1939) was an illustrator to consider. His quaint pen, ink, and watercolor drawings illustrating the gamut of English, Continental, and American fairy tales and legends, including his turn-of-the-century *Fairy Tales of the Brothers Grimm*, were familiar throughout the English-reading world. Word around the Disney studio was that Rackham had been invited to contribute to *Snow White and the Seven Dwarfs*, but at age sixty-eight he was too frail and too fixedly retired in his English countryside cottage to accept.[58] For obvious reasons, German sources were even more influential, particularly since the Swiss-born Hurter was possessed of a "Black Forest type of mind."[59]

Hurter's cottage for the seven dwarfs, hidden deep in an impenetrable forest, found its

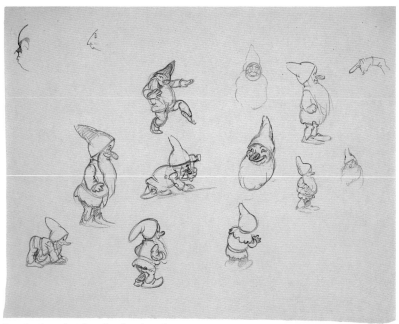

Inspiration sketches for the dwarfs by Albert Hurter

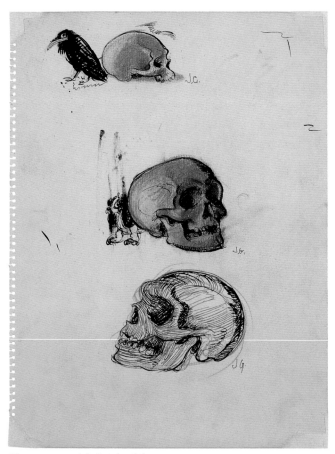

Character model sketch of the raven by Joe Grant

Model sketches of Snow White by Grim Natwick, 1935–36

prototype in the drawings of Ludwig Richter (1803–1884) and in those of his pupil Hermann Vogel (1854–1921), who in the 1890s had illustrated the Grimms' tales in color. Vogel's renditions of richly carved Bavarian woodwork and hand-hewn furniture reappeared in Hurter's inspirational sketches.[60] Hurter's first pencil renderings of the wizened, bearded, gnome-like dwarfs had their antecedents among the folk created by the Swedish illustrator John Bauer (1882–1918),[61] who between 1907 and 1915 had invented a darkly forested world of earthlings in his series *Bland tomtar och troll (Among the Elves and Trolls)*. After him the illustrations were made by his countryman Gustaf Tenggren (1896–1970), who in 1936 was hired by Disney for the latter stages of *Snow White*.[62]

The figure of the Queen was sketched as both a fat, comedic cartoon type and as a stately, beautiful type.[63] Hurter and Grant brought her to her final form, with a face as coldly beautiful as the masks of Wladyslaw T. Benda, whose creations had been the first suggested model in the August 9, 1934, outline. Grant also designed the Queen-as-witch and her raven companion, for whom he acknowledges his debt to Wilhelm Busch's 1867 drawings of *Hans Huckebein, der Unglücksrabe (Jack Crook, Bird of Evil)*.[64]

The figure of Snow White was also evolving throughout 1935. Following the shortcomings of Ham Luske's Persephone in *The Goddess of Spring*, Disney brought in a specialist in human figure animation. He hired Grim Natwick away from Max Fleischer's New York studio, where he had drawn the character of Betty Boop, and put him to work on a Silly Symphony, *The Cookie Carnival* (released May 25, 1935). Natwick then began to define and animate Snow White. His early model drawings of her show a girl with large, widely spaced eyes, pursed lips, and little chin. He experimented with various coiffures and hair colors, including red and blond, which directly contravened the Grimm brothers' description of her with "hair as black as ebony." Natwick's model drawings of Snow White looked like Betty Boop, and they put him at odds with Luske, who had earned the right to be the presumptive head animator of the character.

Luske thought of Snow White as very young—perhaps somewhere between the pre-teenager of the Grimms' story and the fourteen-year-old of the first Disney outlines—because such an age would be easier to animate.[65] Natwick wanted a more mature girl. Disney, recognizing the fact that in his story the princess would fall in love, decreed that she must look old enough to do so.[66] Like Solomon, he later divided the major animating duties among the two men and Natwick's erstwhile assistant, Jack Campbell.[67]

The configurations of the dwarfs were also in flux in 1935. Hurter had made the first pencil renderings, but it was up to the animators to make the final model drawings. "This of course was necessary," says character modeler Grant, "because they were going to animate them. We stretched their imaginations by

Model drawing of Doc by Fred Moore

Gag suggestions for Jumpy, Doc, and Bashful by Earl Hurd, 1935

Dopey

giving them things they couldn't animate, and they would break them down."[68] Disney handed Hurter's sketches of the dwarfs to Fred Moore, with the instruction to give them more personality.[69]

Moore outlined the dwarfs on model sheets to be used by the other animators as preliminary guides from which to draw. On his original model sheet of 1935, the dwarfs remain in the state described in the cast of characters of 1934.[70] Doc is bespeckled, Sleepy lounges in a chair, Happy is fat, Grumpy has a big nose, Deafy cocks his hand to his ear, and Jumpy is beady-eyed. Bashful is baby-faced, big-eared, and undersized. His high-peaked hat covers his baldness, and he wears an over-long tunic, all appropriated by Hurter from America's first comic-strip hero, Richard Outcault's 1896 creation *The Yellow Kid*.[71] When, in early 1936, the identities of the seven were finally settled, Jumpy and Deafy were out; Sneezy was in. Bashful took on a different persona, and the features that had been his were given to the last character to come into play, Dopey.[72]

There was no waiting for all these fine points to be resolved. The story and cast outline were clear enough by early 1935 for the studio to begin composing the music, casting for voices, and scripting the picture, which was the necessary prerequisite for layout and animation.

The 1934 outlines had tentatively suggested various radio personalities for the voices: Sterling Holloway for Sleepy, Professor Diddleton D. Wurtle for Happy, Eddie Holden for Biggy-Wiggy (eventually Doc), and Joe Twerp for Jumpy. Though Janet Gaynor had been suggested as a physical model for Snow White, there was no model for her voice. In early 1935 Disney, looking for a fourteen-year-old voice, auditioned over 148 different talents for this pivotal character. Among them was future film star Deanna Durbin, who actually was fourteen years old, but who was thought by Disney to sound too mature. Upon hearing the nineteen-year-old Adriana Caselotti singing "Some Day My Prince Will Come" to Frank Churchill's piano accompaniment, Disney was convinced.[73] It would be a year, however, before the dialogue and songs would be finished and she could return to the studio to record the soundtrack.

The story slowly evolved through a series of conferences attended by Disney, his storymen, and his story sketch artists. They extended the story line to its full length and then broke it down into its sequences and into the general pacing of its scenes and camera shots. Each shot was treated in a thumbnail story sketch that roughed out the action of the characters involved, vaguely suggested the setting of the action, and footnoted its bit of dialogue. These sketches were then pinned in running order upon a floor-to-ceiling, wall-to-wall storyboard. Drawings could be added, deleted, or changed as ideas came progressively into focus. The storyboards constituted the "script" of the film, from which all the production departments—layout, animation, ink and paint, backgrounds, and camera—would work.[74]

During the story meeting of October 31, chaired by Disney, the division of the story into its sixteen major sequences was determined.[75] The bridge between two particular sequences (ultimately numbered 3D and 4A) through a transition from one song to another was discussed in detail. These songs were to be incorporated seamlessly into the storyline rather than interjected abruptly, as was the standard practice in musicals of the day. Disney picks up the story after Snow White has decided to clean up the dwarfs' cottage:

Walt: She has seen the cobwebs on the ceiling—everything needs to be dusted—dishes must be washed—then that would lead into the statement, "there's lots of work to do" and into the song. Change words of the song so they fit in more with Snow White's handing the animals brushes, etc.

She might say, "Pots and pans aren't hard to bear"—pick up pan and give brush and pan to squirrels . . . They take it wryly . . . Snow White: "If you just hum a merry tune"—and then they start humming—instead of the birds humming.

Then Snow White would start to tell them to "Whistle while you work." She would start giving the animals things to do. . . .

Get a way to finish the song that isn't just an end. . . truck out and the melody of "Whistle While You Work" gets quieter and quieter . . . leave them all working—birds scrubbing clothes—the last thing you see as you truck away is little birds hanging up clothes . . . fade out on that and music would fade

Storyboard drawing for the "Bed-Building Sequence"

Cel setup on a preliminary background for Snow White

out (at the end all you would hear is the flute) before fading into the "Dig, Dig" song and the hammering rhythm.[76]

With the story progressing, Disney began assembling his production team. He brought to the feature his best directors from the shorts: Dave Hand as supervising director, and Perce Pearce, William Cottrell, Wilfred Jackson, Ben Sharpsteen, and lyricist Larry Morey as individual sequence directors. In late 1935 Disney divided the characters among four supervising animators: Ham Luske would be in charge of Snow White and the Prince, Fred Moore and Vladimir Tytla were given the dwarfs, and Norm Ferguson would oversee the Witch.[77] Just as Disney cast his characters, he essentially cast the animators who would bring them to life. "If he gave Grumpy to Tytla— Tytla *was* a grumpy character," Joe Grant observes; "whoever did Happy *was* a happy character. Walt figured it all out for himself."[78] Though Disney recognized the obvious value and necessity of this division of labor, he remained directly involved with every aspect—"night and day, night and day, Walt lived every sprocket hole of this film."[79]

The Stage

1936

Seventeen shorts were released in 1936, but as the year unfolded, more and more of the experienced artists were drained from the shorts and put onto *Snow White* as the studio geared up for production.[80] "With Walt enraptured by the feature," animator Frank Thomas asserts, "you didn't want to be left on the shorts if you could help it."[81]

When a sequence had been storyboarded and okayed for production, it was handed over to its sequence director, who, with the music director, took it to "the music room." Here the length of each scene, its dialogue, and the tempo of its background score were determined and timed into feet of film footage. This ensured that what the audience saw would be synchronized with what they heard.[82] The story was then handed over to the Layout Department, where the picture was staged.

Whereas a story sketch artist could draw in a rudimentary fashion, the layout man had to visualize the staging completely, in miniature, and that, says layout artist Ken O'Connor, "is an all-engaging proposition."[83] Hurter provided the department with inspirational drawings of props, architecture, and backgrounds. Gustaf Tenggren, who came to Disney as an art director in 1936, also began producing inspirational drawings in layout. His work on the feature was limited to two late-developing, darkly dramatic sequences, Snow White's flight through the nightmarish forest, modeled after the montage of MGM's 1931 psychological thriller *Private Worlds*,[84] and the dwarfs' pursuit of the Witch, laid out by Ken O'Connor.[85] While Tenggren is usually given equal credit with Hurter for stylizing the picture, Joe Grant sets the record straight:

> Tenggren was more peripheral. He wasn't in on it at the beginning. He more or less embellished it from the outside. His concepts of the stuff were excellent, beautiful illustration, but they weren't there at the beginning—I wish they were.[86]

The layout artists took these concepts and elaborated them into hundreds of penciled, miniaturized sets upon which the characters would act. Ken Anderson constructed a scale model of the dwarfs' cottage to help him stage the action and gauge camera angles.[87] The layout artists first broke down the storyboards into specific scenes and made rough thumbnail pencil drawings, adding substance to the story sketches. At the same time they made rough layout drawings upon which the camera mechanics— close-ups, long shots, pans—were diagrammed in red pencil for use by the animators. These were followed by finely detailed layout designs made either to serve as precise models for the background painters or as exact outlines over which the animators would lay their paper and plot their animation across the scene.[88]

Anticipating the complexity of picturing *Snow White*'s far more natural environment, peopled with more characters than ever before, the studio went to the considerable expense of increasing the largest size of their Hammermill Management Bond paper stock from 9½ by 12 inches to 12½ by 16 inches. They also repunched the sheets with three holes and two bars rather than the previous two holes to keep the drawings pegged to the animators' boards in more perfect register.[89] This necessitated equipping the layout, animation, background, ink and paint, and camera departments with new drawing boards.

The first scenes began coming out of layout early in 1936, and the animators were ready to begin pilot animation, even if the characters remained imperfectly configured. Luske, who had been entrusted with the most difficult character, Snow White, was the first to get to work. He was followed in March by Fred Moore and then Bill Tytla on the dwarfs, and finally Art Babbitt on the Queen, and Norm Ferguson on the Witch.[90]

Atmosphere watercolor of the dwarfs' cottage

Master layout drawing of a trail through the mountains

*Layout tracing of the sink
in the dwarfs' cottage*

Since Adriana Caselotti had not as yet been brought back to the studio to record the dialogue, Luske borrowed Betty Lawyer (soon to be Mrs. Ward Kimball) from the Ink and Paint Department to read from the script and have her voice recorded on wax records that he could work from.[91] Simultaneously she performed some of Snow White's movements, as preordained in layout, and was filmed for the benefit of Luske's test animation.[92]

Her tasks were soon assumed by Caselotti, who early in the year spent forty-eight days recording the songs and dialogue,[93] and by the teenaged Marjorie Belcher, who walked through Snow White's movements in front of a camera. This film was then run through the "rotoscope" of the studio's invention, which projected the film frame by frame onto a drawing table, where each frame was traced onto animation paper. This tedious task was performed with initial disaffection for the first few months of 1936 by Ken O'Connor: "I did two hundred tracings a day, which then went to the animator, who had a good time changing them."[94] Disney was able to otherwise convince him. He pointed out that O'Connor's tedious labor, hour after hour in his windowless "black hole," was equal to an invaluable education in the mechanics of human motion, an education that the senior animators received only occasionally in Graham's classes.

All the "human" characters (generally those drawn with five fingers rather than four)—Snow White, the Prince, the Queen, the Huntsman, and the Witch—were rotoscoped because they, unlike the dwarfs, had to be constantly lifelike and to always move like humans. The rotoscope was Disney's practical application of Graham's theoretical class in action analysis. It was instituted to mitigate Disney's greatest concern in the film: "None of us knew how those drawings of human figures on the screen were going to be taken. We were prepared for any sort of ridicule."[95] In the end, rotoscope tracings proved to be theoretically sensible, but of little use to the animators.

The direct application of the rotoscope tracings was problematic from the outset. Marjorie Belcher did not (indeed could not) look the way Snow White had been envisioned. An animator might be instructed by the costume movement or take Belcher's nose as a point of reference, but Snow White's eyes were lower on the face, her mouth higher, and her hips narrower.[96] Snow White was to be drawn five heads tall, while Belcher had the normal human proportion of eight heads tall. Furthermore, as O'Connor observed, when one tried to animate by relying exclusively on the rotoscope tracings, "the animation looked as stilted as the devil. It's a funny thing in animation. You have to go further than normal to make it *seem* normal. You have to exaggerate."[97]

It was a costly lesson, but rotoscoping was of only incidental value to many animators. Of one hundred tracings handed him, Grim Natwick said he used perhaps two, the first and the last.[98] He ended up animating much of Snow White and the Prince from experience, but he was one of a select few who wanted to attempt it. "Nobody liked to work on Snow White, she was too exacting," says Ward Kimball, "so Disney picked out guys like Grim Natwick and Jack Campbell, who liked to do girls, and they had the attention to detail that they enjoyed, but nobody else did."[99]

The figure of the Prince, mimed by Louis Hightower and given voice by Harry Stockwell, proved most difficult to handle convincingly. His role was therefore reduced to a few scenes at the beginning and end of the film. Moroni Olsen became the voice of the Magic Mirror, and Stuart Buchanan recorded the Huntsman. Veteran stage and screen actress Lucille LaVerne was invited to record the Queen's voice after Disney had noted her portrayal of the sinister La Vengeance in David O. Selznick's 1935 *A Tale of Two Cities*. She also provided the voice for the withered Witch. Her change of voice alone, accomplished according to Joe Grant by the removal of her false teeth, sparked the development of the Witch's character model.[100] The dwarfs were given voice at this time by Pinto Colvig (Sleepy and Grumpy), Roy Atwell (Doc), Otis Harlan (Happy), Scotty Mattraw (Bashful), and Billy Gilbert (Sneezy). Dopey remained forever voiceless. His personality was to be transmitted by pantomime. How to keep him from seeming imbecilic remained an elusive concept into 1937.[101] Some suggestions came from a baggy-pants, plastic-faced comedian named Eddie Collins,

Rotoscope photograph of the Queen

Original inspiration sketch for the Witch by Joe Grant, 1936

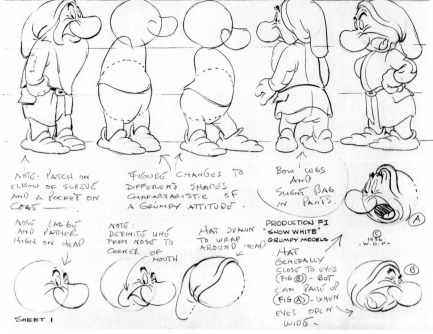

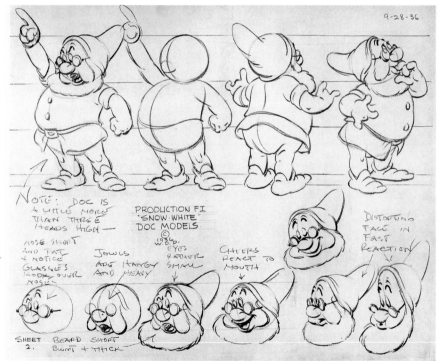

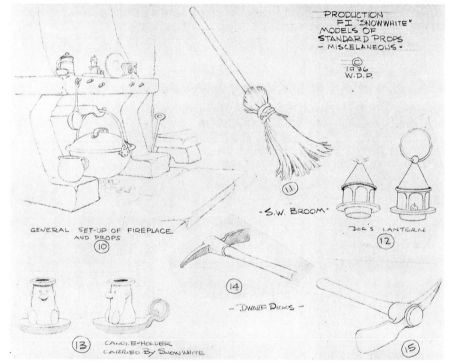

Four photocopies of model sheets, September 28, 1936

discovered in early 1936 by Ward Kimball at a burlesque house in Los Angeles and invited to the studio to be filmed in action.[102]

The animators could assimilate all the clues provided by the story, the character models, the live-action films, and the recorded voices, but it was up to them, as Ham Luske counseled new animators, to turn them into actors:

> Our actors are drawings.
> We cannot work on the inspiration of the moment as an actor does, but must present our characterizations through a combination of art technique and mechanics that takes months from conception to the finished product. And we have to make the audience forget that these are drawings. We cannot risk ruining a sequence or a good characterization with some mechanical imperfection or jitter that reminds the audience that we are dealing with drawings rather than real human beings.[103]

The endowment of a drawn character with a personality was an additive process that did not end until animation was completed, but the physical outlines of the characters of Snow White and the seven dwarfs reached their final configurations on September 28, 1936.

On a comprehensive body of model sheets, all bearing this date, the aspects of these characters—their physical features, costumes, props, and relative height to one another—were standardized. These sheets were photocopied for distribution to all involved animators, suggesting that on that date the period of trial animation ended and the year of full-scale production began.

The precise end or beginning of anything during the making of *Snow White* was relative. No department's work was completely done before another's could begin. While some sequences were ready to animate in the last months of 1936, others were still in the Story Department.[104] But Disney was beginning to look ahead to the end product, and on December 1 he expressed the following thoughts on color:

> We want to imagine it as rich as we can without splashing color all over the place. I saw Harman-Ising's cartoon about Spring . . . last night. They got colors everywhere and it looks cheap. There is nothing subtle about it at all. It's just poster-like. A lot of people think that's what a cartoon should have. I think we are trying to achieve something different here. We are not going after comic supplement coloring. We have to strive for a certain depth and realism . . . the subduing of the colors at the right time and for the right effect.[105]

Such color decisions were to be made in the Background Department and in the Ink and Paint Department. Theirs were the last pieces completed before the picture was committed to camera.

Production

Disney's assessment of his feature's prospects in 1937 was tempered by a few lingering doubters within his own company and by a host of naysayers outside:

> You should have heard the howls of warning when we started making a full-length cartoon. It was prophesied that nobody would sit through such a thing. But there was only one way we could do it successfully and that was to plunge ahead and go for broke—shoot the works. There could be no compromising on money, talent, or time.[106]

As the rumors of the money, talent, and time he had already expended on such an untested commodity leaked from the studio, the feature earned the epithet "Disney's Folly"—which was its presumed epitaph as well. And the amount already expended was nothing compared to the money, talent, and time that Disney was prepared to spend in production in 1937. All the talk made his bankers nervous, and they pressured him to set a release date.[107] They settled on the end of the year.

The scope of the venture the studio faced can be assessed from the magnitude of the numbers involved. The final drafts of the script for each sequence, typed for distribution in the months between January 5 and December 2, 1937, reveal the sheer quantity of the work at hand (Appendix B).

The film was divided into sixteen numbered sequences, from which Sequence 12 and parts of Sequences 1 and 14 had already been dropped. The remaining fifteen were subdivided into lettered subsequences. In these sequences there was an aggregate of 780 scenes, from which 51 had been deleted by the time the drafts were typed. Many of the remaining scenes were, like the sequences, further subdivided into lettered subscenes. Each scene was assigned an animator, a background, and its predetermined length of screen footage, timed to 1/100th of a foot. When combined, the drafts' figures total 8,196 running feet of film. When calculated at the standard rate of 90 feet of film per minute, a film of this length would run 91 minutes.

If there were to be only one animation drawing and its one corresponding hand-inked and painted cel for each 24th of a second in each of these 91 minutes, the total number of drawings (and cels) would be 131,040. However, much of *Snow White* was animated on four overlaying cel levels. The total number of drawings and cels might therefore be multiplied fourfold to 524,160. No one in 1937 stopped to count the actual numbers of drawings and cels used in the production, but 250,000 was an early estimate.[108]

If one animator had been given the whole job and had worked at the accepted average rate of 160 drawings per week, producing 10 feet of film in the six-day workweek,[109] his task would have taken 819 weeks to complete.

If one inker had been given the sole responsibility of tracing these animation drawings onto celluloid at the studio's standard rate of 30 cels a day, producing 1.3 feet of film,[110] her job (for all the inkers and painters were women) would have consumed 6,305 working days, or 1,261 five-day workweeks (to which the women were limited).[111]

If one woman had painted all of these cels in gouache at the studio's estimated rate of 17 cels a day, or 1.1 feet of film,[112] it would have taken her 1,490 weeks, the equivalent of 29 years.

If one background painter had produced each fully detailed watercolor background (as was generally required for each of the finalized 729 scene changes in the film) at a rate of one per day, he would have been at work for 121 weeks.

If one cameraman had been assigned to photograph all the accumulated cels on their

Cel setup of the dwarfs' bedroom (Sequence 4C, Scene 15)

Atmosphere drawing for The Old Mill *by Maurice Noble, 1937*

Snow White window bill
designed by Gustaf Tenggren

backgrounds (cel setups), and if he worked at the studio's average speed of 96 cel setups, or 6 feet of film, per hour,[113] it would have taken him 1,366 hours, or 28 weeks, to transfer the drawings to film.

Yet from January 5 only 50 weeks remained for all these departments to accomplish and synchronize their parts.

There was not just one animator but 32, and distributed among them were 102 assistant animators and 107 inbetweeners.[114] There was not one inker or one painter, but 66 and 178, respectively.[115] There was not one cameraman, but several, who were split into two crews working on at least two camera stands. In all 750 artists are said to have contributed to the feature between 1934 and 1937,[116] making it the largest collaborative art project ever undertaken in the United States. Background painter Maurice Noble aptly characterizes the final year of production as "a period of a series of nervous breakdowns."[117]

Both time and money were in short supply, and Disney was flying by the seat of his pants. Neither shortage prevented him from lavishing both commodities on every detail of production. He was constantly looking over shoulders and had a propensity to change his mind when presented with as simple a thing as a new drawing. "We never knew if the studio would still be going the next week," admits Frank Thomas. "Our big concern was that Walt would go off in some crazy direction and kill the whole idea of the thing. . . and Walt would change his mind very often, and usually stick with an idea for one whole day. And then he'd come up with a new

idea that was twice as good as the one he'd had before, and he'd get you all sold on that."[118]

Disney encouraged new ideas for the feature. Innovations came from all departments and were put into practice in 1937. From the Camera Department came the multiplane camera, invented by production manager Bill Garity. Whereas the standard camera stand was fixed, the multiplane had moveable cel levels that could be independently adjusted up or down, toward or away from the camera. These adjustments heightened the illusion of a third dimension on the screen. Disney spent $75,000 on this technology.[119] He tested it in *The Old Mill,* an Academy Award-winning Silly Symphony released on November 5, 1937, just a month in advance of the feature.

The Old Mill was a mood piece and largely the product of the recently confederated Special Effects Department. Its animators created everything from raindrops to wind to shadows which, prior to 1935, had been rendered by the character animators as obvious clichés.[120] *The Old Mill*'s potent thunderstorm was a trial run for the natural and unnatural phenomena in *Snow White.*

To achieve the new subtlety of color Disney desired, the backgrounds for *Snow White* were all painted in grayed-down transparent watercolors rather than the vivid colors of the shorts. This muted palette was most suitable to the current limitations of Technicolor, which at the time was capable of capturing only mid-range colors.[121] Sam Armstrong supervised the change.

Transparent watercolors, however, have the inherent liability of being unalterable once they are on paper. If an animator, working from the final layout tracing, decided that more time or space was needed for the action at hand, he would add it. The drawing would then go back to layout, where it might have to be changed. This could also necessitate a change in the background, which had been painted from the same original master layout. A finished watercolor background often had to be discarded.

This was but one battle among the departments in the stress-filled studio during 1937. The Story Department posted a sign pointing at the animators, "It was funny when it left here!"[122] Among the animators, the Natwick camp and the Luske camp were constantly at odds. No animator liked the way another was animating the same character in a different scene.[123] Moore's dwarfs were the models of choice, but Tenggren, now separately creating the publicity drawings for the feature's posters and window bills, was picturing the dwarfs after his own fashion, with as much kinship to John Bauer's button-eyed trolls as to Moore's prototypes. This upset Moore.[124]

Disney unconsciously kept the peace, says Marc Davis, by adopting a friendly convention throughout the studio:

> I think the greatest thing that Disney ever did was have everybody called by his first name. He was Walt, I was Marc, you

were Tom, Dick, or Harry. It's hard to get angry at somebody that you're on a first-name basis with. He somehow or other had that intuition. There were only two people who were called "Mister" in the early studio. One was Mr. Rogers. He was a carpenter, in his seventies, and so out of respect for his age, he was called Mr. Rogers. The other was Mr. Keener. Mr. Keener was the paymaster, and he was "Mister" because the studio had trouble raising the money every week for the payroll.[125]

The money problems became critical in mid-production in 1937. Disney recalled the situation years later:

> Then came the shocker. My brother Roy told me that we would have to borrow another quarter of a million dollars to finish the movie. I had to take the bits and pieces [of completed film] to show the bankers as collateral. . . . On the appointed day, I sat alone with Joe Rosenberg of the Bank of America, watching those bits and pieces on a screen, trying to sell him a quarter of a million dollars worth of faith. After the lights came on, he didn't show the slightest reaction to what he'd just seen. He walked out of the projection room, remarked that it was a nice day, and yawned! Then he turned to me and said "Walt, that picture will make a pot full of money."[126]

With the loan secured, Disney went back to work, reinforced.

Storyboard drawing for the "Bed-Building Sequence," 1937

Layout tracing for the "Bed-Building Sequence," 1937

After every drawing from story sketch to finished and cleaned-up animation was approved, each phase was filmed onto reels in "test camera." From these the artist could judge the continuity of his own work and Disney and the directors—sitting in "the sweatbox," a room that the animators found "hot to begin with and then hotter under stress"[127]—could critique the work in progress. Harry Tytle, the test cameraman, reconstructs the process:

> Test camera begins with the story sketches, which were the first steps okayed for production. Then it went to the animator, who did his roughs. These formed the test reels that the director could look at and make his changes. And then, when he thought it was right, he'd call Walt in, and Walt would look at it and say, I want this changed or that changed or I want more personality in it. Then it was okayed and would go to clean-up animation. Then, that was okayed for inking and painting. At the same time the background was being painted. Then it would go to the Camera Department. The camera would shoot it. Then you would get a daily and you would see it. And that's it! When you got a whole combination of dailies put together, you had a finished picture.[128]

Even with the deadline looming, Disney made major alterations in the final months of production. He had a natural feeling for what ought to be in the story, and he added and subtracted scenes to advance the plot. One sequence was elaborated by intercutting additional animation. Disney explained the addition to animator Ollie Johnston, "When Snow White and the dwarfs are having that entertainment, and she's singing 'Some Day My Prince Will Come,' the audience will want that to last forever, because the Witch is coming!"[129]

His first edits hit the cutting room floor in 1937. The "Soup-Eating Symphony," the second part of Sequence 6, the follow-up to the dwarfs washing at the tub, had been integral to the story since 1934 and was still actively discussed by Disney in the last week of 1936. Two months later its draft script was finalized, and Ward Kimball spent the next months working out its animation. His rough drawings already had been cleaned up and sent to Ink and Paint when Disney called him into his office and said: "Ward, I don't know how to tell you this, the soup sequence is funny but I've got to take it out. I've been looking at the picture [and he looked at it two or three times a day] and I've got to get back to the wicked queen!"[130] To Kimball (and doubtless to Natwick, who had animated Snow White in these scenes, and to Fred Spencer, Vladimir Tytla, Les Clark, Dick Lundy, and Bill Roberts, who had joined Kimball in animating the dwarfs), "it was like getting hit with a custard pie."[131] The cuts were painful to them, and painful and expensive to Disney. "When the animator gets the story, and it gets into animation," Frank Thomas observes, "now *that* gets expensive.

So you don't want to change any more than you have to. But, on your first feature, you *absolutely* have to."[132]

Next to go were the "Lodge Meeting," in which the dwarfs decide to build a bed for Snow White, and the following "Bed Building" (Sequence 11 A&B). Their scripts had been finalized in the drafts of October and November 1937. They had advanced to filmed "pencil test" animation, where they still exist, but they did not make it into the film. To Disney this funny interlude interrupted the Witch's journey to Snow White's cottage, and so he deleted it.

To further tighten the drama, individual scenes were edited. Scenes 36 to 46 of Sequence 5A, featuring a bedroom brawl between Doc and Grumpy following the discovery of Snow White asleep on their beds had been animated by Fred Moore and cleaned up by Ollie Johnston, and their backgrounds had been painted by the time Disney cut them. He was irked by the squabbling.[133] The first half-minute of the Witch preparing the poison apple (Sequence 9A, Scenes 1-1AD), featuring the animation of Norm Ferguson and the work of the Special Effects Department, was also dropped.

Given Disney's general abhorrence of everything ugly, his staff found it interesting that he let the Queen's total villainy pass untouched.[134] And he let her die, implicitly. While he personally disliked this scenario, he knew, as Johnston says, that "she was right for the picture, but he never wanted to do anything like that again."[135] The evil incarnated in the Queen

Animation rough and its layout tracing for the "Bed-Building Sequence," 1937

transformed the original concept of a gagfest starring the seven dwarfs into the ultimate "murder story" starring Snow White as the innocent victim.[136] "The Soup-Eating Symphony," "Lodge Meeting," and "Bed Building" all stopped this story, so they were left on the cutting room floor.[137]

Disney's five deletions cut one-seventh of the film's projected running footage, from 8,196 feet to 7,000 feet, or the equivalent of 13 minutes. Instead of 91 minutes, the animated portions of the film ran 78 minutes. When joined by the opening credits and the story's introduction via the turning pages of the storybook, the film reached its final 83 minutes.

The premiere was set for December; the animators were still drawing in September.[138] Most of the backgrounds were okayed for production with the "OK SA" (Sam Armstrong) stamp of approval in August, September, October, and into November. In these months, nearly everyone was working fifteen-hour days, the women from 6 am to 9 pm and the men from 7 am to 10 pm.[139] By October the final two links in the production chain, Ink and Paint and Camera, were working in shifts around the clock.[140]

No one on staff was paid overtime, but they were given thirty-five-cent meal tickets, which they spent at the restaurant across the street, where they gathered to commiserate.[141] Beyond that, there was no socializing between the male employees and the women in the Ink and Paint Department cloistered in the Annex.

In November the quarter-million-dollar loan was exhausted. Some staff carried on with reduced or deferred pay.[142] Disney occasionally ran the dailies for the staff to keep up enthusiasm,[143] but they were barely enough to allay concerns about how it would all come out.

Even Disney, who alone had a total grasp of the picture, had worries: "I began to have some doubts, too, if we could ever get our investment back."[144] He had invested $1,480,000, more than four times the average cost for an American feature film in 1937.[145]

The premiere at the Carthay Circle Theatre on the evening of December 21 was a gathering of Hollywood's glitterati—Chaplin, Garland, Barrymore, Gable and Lombard. Mingling with them were the anonymous makers of the film— select storymen, layout artists, background painters, and animators—to whom Disney had given tickets.[146] There was great anticipation, for although they knew the worth of their work, they could not know how the audience would react. They shared the specter of *The Drunkard*, an enduring melodrama, at which the audience was urged to hiss and boo the villain.[147] As Ward Kimball remembers the evening:

> As I look back on it, we knew where they were going to laugh from experience, but we weren't prepared for the crying and sniffing in the audience. That was the thing I started hearing. Clark Gable and Carole Lombard were sitting close, and when Snow White was poisoned, stretched out on that slab, they started blowing their

noses. I could hear it— crying—that was the big surprise. We worried about the serious stuff and whether they would feel for this girl, and when they did, I knew it was in the bag. Everybody did.[148]

Disney still was not quite satisfied. He noticed a flaw in the animation of the Prince as he bent to kiss Snow White, which caused a virtually imperceptible jitter, and he wanted it fixed. Most chroniclers of the film state that Roy Disney dissuaded his brother because of the cost in dollars that were no longer there.[149] But a contemporary account in *Liberty* states that "even after the film was running in New York, he was still working on new animation for the Prince. He sent it on too, and made the theaters use it."[150]

Epilogue

1938

Snow White and the Seven Dwarfs was an immediate and unqualified popular and critical success in general release. At New York's cavernous Radio City Music Hall, "where no film has ever played more than three weeks," *Snow White* ran for five, "with greater and greater crowds coming every week."[151]

The nation's critics, voting in *The Film Daily*, named *Snow White and the Seven Dwarfs* the "best film of the year," ahead of nine other memorable films of 1938, including *You Can't Take It With You, Alexander's Ragtime Band, Boys' Town,* and *The Adventures of Robin Hood.* It placed second to *The Citadel* on the "ten best" list published by the New York Film Critics; it won a special award from the National Board of Review; and it won for Disney a special Oscar consisting of one big and seven little statues.[152]

In recognition of his dual contributions, Disney was awarded a Master of Science by the University of California and a Master of Arts by Yale in the summer of 1938.[153] But there was little time for him or anyone else at the studio to rest on the laurels, since the next two features, *Pinocchio* and *Bambi,* were already on the drawing boards. These pictures and the brand new Disney Studio in Burbank were

being built on the revenues generated by *Snow White and the Seven Dwarfs.* As Disney's banker had predicted, it made "a whole pot full of money."

Some estimates placed the film's 1938 revenues at ten million dollars from both foreign and domestic release, making it the most successful film ever made.[154] Spin-off enterprises, which had been anticipated during production, were in full spin by the official release date of February 4, 1938:

> The by-products, reproductions of the Dwarfs and Snow White, are selling up into the hundreds of thousands of dollars, fashioned in every substance from platinum to soap, from charm bracelets to sweat shirts. Snow White dresses for children are in all the department stores; Snow White toys are all over; Snow White books are crowding the cosmetics out of drugstores; Snow White songs are on the air, in record sets, selling in thousands of copies as sheet music. There are even Snow White hams and bacons coming on the market. And that's only the beginning. Remember, the film isn't yet four months old.[155]

As part of this popular marketing, indeed its most interesting part, the Walt Disney Studios contracted with the Courvoisier Art Galleries of San Francisco to globally distribute

components of the film—a selection of drawings, cels, and backgrounds—which had no further function once they had been photographed for the film. While the animation drawings went into an archive for reference, the majority of the cels were discarded, washed off, or destroyed. But in August 1938 seven thousand of them were saved for the initial sale to museums and the public through the nation's art galleries.[156] This was reportedly done in response to the demand from fans, who wanted to hold a piece of what had had such a fleeting existence on the screen. The precedent for preserving the best of the cels and cel setups, however, had been set by Disney in his gallery and museum shows of 1932–34.

These bits and pieces proved a democratic form of art. They were equally appreciated by adults and children, by the man on the street and the museum curator. This had been a virtue of the film itself, in the opinion of the constant Disney champion, Dorothy Grafly: "There will be hundreds of thousands of men, women and children in American motion picture theaters who will receive their baptism in art through the magic of Walt Disney. . . . In Walt Disney's animated cartoons art comes to the man."[157]

Gustaf Tenggren's poster design for Snow White, *1937*

Divorced from their contexts of motion and sound, the component drawings were but imperfect parts of the whole. One could even say they were faulty representatives, given that the film's impact depended on the audience's oblivion to the fact that they were watching a constant stream of individual drawings. But the preserved cel setups proved that each of the film's frames was a fully satisfactory universe in its own right. Through them, and through the whole corpus of preliminary drawings, the care and artistry that went into each 24th of a second of *Snow White* could be perfectly understood and appreciated. The pieces proved as fascinating to the public as the whole.

In 1940 the Los Angeles County Museum organized a *Retrospective Exhibition of the Walt Disney Medium.* It was a complete overview of twelve years of Disney artistry, from *Steamboat Willie* through *Fantasia*, as told through the gamut of drawings from preliminary story sketches to backgrounds and cels. The exhibition traveled from Los Angeles to the University Gallery in Minneapolis, the Cincinnati Art Museum, the St. Louis City Art Museum, the Art Institute of Chicago, the Detroit Institute of Arts, the Cleveland Museum of Art, and the Worcester Art Museum. The purpose of the exhibition, its catalogue stated, was to bear witness to a considerable achievement: "In twelve years Walt Disney has elevated animated pictures from a crude form of entertainment to the dignity of a true art. No other medium has such plasticity."[158] *The Art Digest* gave credit to the director of the Los Angeles County Museum, Roland J. McKinney, for doing what art museum directors ought to do: "He is helping to make his museum a more vital part of his community by bringing to it greater understanding of a new art medium."[159]

Notes

Overture

1. Ollie Johnston, interview with the author, February 20, 1994.
2. Dorothy Grafly, "America's Youngest Art," *The American Magazine of Art* 26:7 (July 1933):337.
3. "A New Art in the Making," *The Art News* 31:15 (January 7, 1933):2.

Opening Credits—1933

4. Bob Thomas, *Walt Disney: An American Original* (New York: Simon and Schuster, 1976), p. 123.
5. Ibid., p. 86.
6. Ibid., pp. 102, 113.
7. Miriam Stillwell, "The Story Behind Snow White's $10,000,000 Surprise Party," *Liberty* (April 9, 1938):8.
8. Kevin Brownlow, *The Parade's Gone By* (New York: Bonanza Books, 1968), p. 217.
9. Robert D. Feild, *The Art of Walt Disney* (New York: The Macmillan Company, 1942), p. 67.
10. *The International Encyclopedia of Film*, ed. Dr. Roger Manvell (New York: Crown Publishers, 1972), p. 31.
11. Dorothy Grafly "America's Youngest Art," *The American Magazine of Art* 26:7 (July 1933):338.
12. Quoted in Thomas, *Walt Disney: An American Original*, p. 204.
13. Ibid., p. 116.
14. Quoted in Robin Allan, "The fairest film of all: *Snow White* reassessed," *Animator* 21 (October–December 1987):20.

15. Richard Holliss and Brian Sibley, *Walt Disney's Snow White and the Seven Dwarfs & the Making of the Classic Film* (New York: Simon & Schuster, Inc., 1987), p. 5.
16. Christopher Finch, *The Art of Walt Disney* (New York: Abrams, 1973), p. 65.
17. *Retrospective Exhibition of the Walt Disney Medium* (Los Angeles County Museum, 1940), n. p.
18. Disney won this award every year from its inception in 1932 through the end of the decade. Subsequent winners were *The Tortoise and the Hare* (1934), *Three Orphan Kittens* (1935), *Country Cousin* (1936), *The Old Mill* (1937), *Ferdinand, the Bull* (1938), and *The Ugly Duckling* (1939).
19. Thomas, *Walt Disney: An American Original*, p. 123.
20. Ward Kimball, interview with the author, February 22, 1994.
21. Frank Thomas, interview with the author, February 20, 1994.
22. *Retrospective Exhibition of the Walt Disney Medium*. Howard Green, "Epics of Animation: *Snow White and the Seven Dwarfs*," *Cinemagic* 36 (1987):41, establishes the initial budget at $150,000. Bob Thomas, *Walt Disney: An American Original*, p. 130, says $500,000.
23. Walt Disney, "Snow White," *Showplace, The Magazine of Radio City Music Hall* 2:3 (January 20, 1938):14.

The Story—1934

24. Walt Disney "Snow White," *Showplace, The Magazine of Radio City Music Hall* 2:3 (January 20, 1938):7.
25. Richard Holliss and Brian Sibley, *Walt Disney's Snow White and the Seven Dwarfs & the Making of the Classic Film* (New York: Simon & Schuster, Inc., 1987), p. 6.
26. Miriam Stillwell, "The Story Behind Snow White's $10,000,000 Surprise Party," *Liberty* (April 9, 1938):8.

27. Daniel Blum, *A Pictorial History of the American Theatre 1860–1970* (New York: Crown Publishers, Inc., 1969), p. 132.
28. Disney, "Snow White," p. 7.
29. Ibid., pp. 7, 14.
30. Joe Grant, interview with the author, February 21, 1994.
31. Ward Kimball, interview with the author, February 22, 1994.
32. Bob Thomas, *Walt Disney: An American Original* (New York: Simon and Schuster, 1976), p. 133.
33. Frank Thomas, interview with the author, February 20, 1994.
34. Holliss and Sibley, *Walt Disney's Snow White*, p. 12–13.
35. *Snow White (tentative outline)*, October 22, 1934, typescript, p. 1, Ison Collection.
36. Ibid., p. 2.
37. In an interesting reversal, the Prince's imprisonment in the Queen's dungeon, his aided escape, and his rush to the rescue on his intelligent white charger, all proposed in these early outlines for *Snow White*, were eventually dropped, but they reappear in Disney's *Sleeping Beauty* (1959).
38. *Snow White (Brief Outline for Gag Suggestions)*, November 6, 1934, typescript, pp. 3, 7.
39. Disney, "Snow White," p. 14.

Sequence—1935

40. Bob Thomas, *Walt Disney: An American Original* (New York: Simon and Schuster, 1976), p. 128.
41. Ibid., p. 124.
42. Frank Thomas and Ollie Johnston, interviews with the author, February 20, 1994.
43. Frank Thomas interview.
44. Ward and Betty Kimball, interviews with the author, February 22, 1994;

confirmed by Marc Davis (interview with the author, February 21, 1994), though he started with a contract of $22.50 a week because of his added ability to draw animals. Joe Grant, an established caricaturist, started in 1933 at $75 a week (interview with the author, February 21, 1994). Dinner at "Charlie's," the neighborhood café, was 35 cents.

45. Quoted in Thomas, *Walt Disney: An American Original*, p. 125.

46. Frank Thomas interview.

47. Ibid.

48. Ward Kimball interview.

49. Frank Thomas interview.

50. Ollie Johnston interview.

51. Maurice Noble, interview with the author, February 21, 1994.

52. Betty Kimball interview.

53. Quoted in Robin Allan, "The fairest film of all: *Snow White* reassessed," *Animator* 21 (October-December 1987):18.

54. Quoted in Howard Green, "Epics of Animation: Snow White and the Seven Dwarfs," *Cinemagic* 36 (1987):42. Though this and other articles place the meeting in 1934, this is not only improbable, since Anderson was only an inbetweener in the summer of 1934, but actually impossible, since Ollie Johnston and Marc Davis, who were not hired until 1935, also attended. Frank Thomas, correspondence with the author, April 21, 1994.

55. Richard Holliss and Brian Sibley, *Walt Disney's Snow White and the Seven Dwarfs & the Making of the Classic Film* (New York: Simon & Schuster, Inc., 1987), p. 15.

56. Joe Grant, interview with the author, February 21, 1994.

57. Ibid.

58. This invitation was reported by Don Graham to Frank Thomas; interview with the author, February 20, 1994; Joe Grant has no recollection of this invitation.

59. Ken O'Connor, interview with the author, February 24, 1994.

60. Joe Grant interview.

61. Ibid.

62. Per Bjorström, *Bauer, En Konstnär och hans Sagovärld* (Stockholm: Nationalmuseum, 1981), p. 159.

63. Holliss and Sibley, *Walt Disney's Snow White*, pp. 10, 12.

64. Joe Grant interview; cf. Walter Arndt, *The Genius of Wilhelm Busch* (Berkeley: University of California Press, 1982), reproduced pp. 36-41.

65. Frank Thomas interview.

66. John Grant, *Encyclopedia of Walt Disney's Animated Characters* (New York: Hyperion, 1993), p. 151.

67. Calculating from the 1937 final drafts of the script, Snow White appears in 229 scenes: 60 are listed as Luske's responsibility, 58 as Natwick's, 74 as Jack Campbell's, and 20 are listed as the dual responsibility of two of the three. The remaining 17 belong to Robert Stokes.

68. Joe Grant interview.

69. Ward Kimball interview.

70. Holliss and Sibley, *Walt Disney's Snow White*, reprod. p. 8.

71. Ward Kimball interview.

72. Frank Thomas and Ollie Johnston, *Disney Animation: The Illusion of Life* (New York: Abbeville Press, 1981), p. 394; reproduction of the "Dopey Model Sheet," dated February 21, 1936.

73. Adriana Caselotti and Brian Sibley, "With a smile and a song," *Animator* 21 (October-December 1987):22.

74. Ralph Hulett, "The Artist's Part in the Production of an Animated Cartoon," *American Artist* 19:5 (May 1955):32.

75. Sequences 11 and 12, originally consigned to the Queen's first attempt on Snow White's life by poisoned comb and

to the Prince's escape from the dungeon, were dropped soon after the division was decided upon. The bed-building scenes were expanded and became Sequence 11. It in turn was dropped in late 1937. Sequence 8B, in which Snow White sings "Some Day My Prince Will Come," was storyboarded as a dream sequence with Snow White dancing with the Prince in the clouds. It was transformed into "storytelling."

76. Quoted in Robert D. Feild, *The Art of Walt Disney* (New York: The Macmillan Company, 1942), pp. 119–20.

77. Thomas and Johnston, *Disney Animation*, p. 93.

78. Joe Grant interview.

79. Frank Thomas interview.

The Stage—1936

80. Jack Hannah, interview with the author, February 19, 1994.

81. Frank Thomas, interview with the author, February 20, 1994.

82. The Disney Gang, "Steps in Animated Cartooning," unidentified magazine clipping, September 1938, Stout Reference Library files, Indianapolis Museum of Art.

83. Ken O'Connor, interview with the author, February 24, 1994.

84. Robin Allan, "The fairest film of all: *Snow White* reassessed," *Animator* 21 (October–December 1987):19.

85. Ken O'Connor interview.

86. Joe Grant, interview with the author, February 21, 1994.

87. Ollie Johnston, interview with the author, February 20, 1994.

88. Maurice Noble, interview with the author, February 21, 1994.

89. The new peg system was in use by the time the short *Moving Day* was in production in June 1936; cf. John Canemaker, *Treasures of Disney Animation Art* (New York: Abbeville Press,

1982), plates 67–71. This is confirmed by Ken O'Connor, who laid out *Moving Day*; correspondence with the author, April 11, 1994.

90. Ollie Johnston interview, and in correspondence April 17, 1994.

91. Betty Kimball, interview with the author, February 22, 1994. She and Ward Kimball were married on August 15, 1936.

92. Ibid.

93. Adriana Caselotti and Brian Sibley, "With a smile and a song," *Animator* 21 (October-December 1987):22.

94. Ken O'Connor interview.

95. Disney to Frank Daugherty, *Christian Science Monitor*, 1938, quoted in John Grant, *Encyclopedia of Walt Disney's Animated Characters* (New York: Hyperion, 1993), p. 152.

96. Ward Kimball interview.

97. Ken O'Connor interview.

98. Robin Allan, "The fairest film of all," p. 21.

99. Ward Kimball interview.

100. Joe Grant interview.

101. Frank Thomas and Ollie Johnston, *Disney Animation: The Illusion of Life* (New York: Abbeville Press, 1981), p. 395.

102. Ward Kimball interview.

103. Quoted in Thomas and Johnston, *Disney Animation*, pp. 113–14.

104. Richard Holliss and Brian Sibley, *Walt Disney's Snow White and the Seven Dwarfs & the Making of the Classic Film* (New York: Simon & Schuster, Inc., 1987), pp. 22-23.

105. Ibid., p. 24.

Production—1937

106. Quoted in Howard Green, "Epics of Animation: Snow White and the Seven Dwarfs," *Cinemagic* 36 (1987):44.

107. Robert D. Feild, *The Art of Walt Disney* (New York: The Macmillan Company, 1942), p. 49.

108. "Inside Story," *Showplace, The Magazine of Radio City Music Hall* 2:3 (January 20, 1938):11.

109. Frank Thomas and Ollie Johnston, *Disney Animation: The Illusion of Life* (New York: Abbeville Press, 1981), p. 317.

110. "Inter-Office Communication," October 15, 1938, Walt Disney Productions, Ltd.

111. Betty Kimball, interview with the author, February 22, 1994.

112. "Inter-Office Communication," October 15, 1938, Walt Disney Productions, Ltd.

113. Figures provided by Walt Disney Productions,"Motion Pictures," *Encyclopedia Britannica* 15 (1949), p. 871.

114. Green, "Epics of Animation," p. 45.

115. "Inter-Office Communication," October 15, 1938, Walt Disney Productions, Ltd.

116. John Grant, *Encyclopedia of Walt Disney's Animated Characters* (New York: Hyperion, 1993), p. 149.

117. Maurice Noble, interview with the author, February 21, 1994.

118. Frank Thomas, interview with the author, February 20, 1994.

119. "Inside Story," *Showplace*, p. 11.

120. Ward Kimball, interview with the author, February 22, 1994.

121. Frank Thomas interview. When Technicolor was used in live action features in the 1940s, the following guide to "make-up application" was published: "No blacks, greens or blues are used. The basic tone of Technicolor make-up is light-gray. When photographed and projected on the screen, it is magnified and the colour intensified. The result of this subdued make-up colouring gives the effect of normal or natural skin." "Motion Pictures," *Encyclopedia Britannica* 15 (1949), p. 863.

122. Frank Thomas interview.

123. Ibid.; and Marc Davis, interview with the author, February 21, 1994.

124. Frank Thomas interview.

125. Marc Davis interview.

126. Quoted in Green, "Epics of Animation," pp. 44–45.

127. Ollie Johnston, interview with the author, February 20, 1994.

128. Harry Tytle, interview with the author, February 23, 1994.

129. Ollie Johnston interview.

130. Ward Kimball interview.

131. Ibid.

132. Frank Thomas interview.

133. Ollie Johnston interview.

134. Ibid.

135. Ibid.; the death of Bambi's mother is a memorable exception to this rule.

136. Ibid.

137. Unlike a live-action film, little is actually "cut" in the editing room from a finished animated feature film. All editing is "pre-visualized" before the expense of animation, inking, painting, and camera is incurred. At the Disney Studios editors were known simply as "cutters" who spliced together the finished lengths of film; Harry Tytle interview.

138. Ollie Johnston interview.

139. Ward and Betty Kimball interviews; Ollie Johnston, correspondence with the author, April 17, 1994.

140. Maurice Noble, interview with the author, February 21, 1994.

141. Betty Kimball interview. When Harry Tytle married Marion, a Disney secretary, on December 31, 1939, they were the thirty-ninth studio couple to be wed; Harry Tytle interview.

142. Marc Davis interview.

143. Betty Kimball interview.

144. Quoted in Green, "Epics of Animation," p. 44.

145. "Motion Pictures," *Encyclopedia Britannica* 15 (1949), p. 858.

146. Adriana Caselotti and Harry Stockwell were not on the list, so they sneaked into the balcony. Adriana Caselotti and Brian Sibley, "With a smile and a song," *Animator* 21 (October–December 1987):23.

147. Ollie Johnston interview.

148. Ward Kimball interview.

149. Richard Holliss and Brian Sibley, *Walt Disney's Snow White and the Seven Dwarfs & the Making of the Classic Film* (New York: Simon & Schuster, Inc., 1987), p. 35.

150. Miriam Stillwell, "The Story Behind Snow White's $10,000,000 Surprise Party," *Liberty* (April 9, 1938):8.

Epilogue—1938

151. Miriam Stillwell, "The Story Behind Snow White's $10,000,000 Surprise Party," *Liberty* (April 9, 1938):8.

152. Paul Michael, *The American Movies: A Pictorial Encyclopedia* (New York: Garland Books, 1969), pp. 367, 372, 378.

153. "Walt Disney, M.S. M.A," *The Art Digest* 12:18 (July 1, 1938):17.

154. Stillwell, "The Story Behind . . . ," p. 8. The actual box-office receipts totaled $8,500,000. Richard Holliss and Brian Sibley, *Walt Disney's Snow White and the Seven Dwarfs & The Making of the Classic Film* (New York: Simon & Schuster, Inc., 1987), p. 66.

155. Stillwell, "The Story Behind . . . ," p. 8.

156. "World-Wide Disney," *Magazine of Art* 31:9 (September 1938):546.

157. "The Magic of Disney," *The Art Digest* 12:13 (April 1, 1938):25.

158. *Retrospective Exhibition of the Walt Disney Medium* (Los Angeles County Museum, 1940) n. p.

159. "Disney Museumized," *The Art Digest* 15:6 (December 15, 1940):11.

Appendix A

Synopsis

Snow White and the Prince fell in love. This fact arouses the Queen's fury. She throws the Prince into a dungeon and orders her Huntsman to take Snow White into the woods and bring back the girl's heart. The Huntsman confesses the plot to Snow White and leaves her to wander in the forest. He will try to fool the Queen by substituting a swine's heart for Snow White's.

Snow White, lost in the woods, comes upon the dwarfs' cottage near sundown. Nobody is home. She enters. The untidy confusion, the small garments on the floor, the seven-of-everything, lead her to the conclusion that seven orphans live there. She and the birds clean house, and, finally, Snow White falls asleep.

The dwarfs return through the woods, singing their marching song. They see the cottage door open and they are startled, indignant, frightened. Someone has been there! They enter. Everything is CLEAN! They search the house and find Snow White asleep. They decide to let her stay, in the face of Grumpy's warnings about the Queen's vengeance and women being bad luck.

Snow White makes the dwarfs go into the yard and wash up while she cooks dinner.

At dinner, Snow White says "grace" and the dwarfs go at the soup with a babble of soup-sucking-sounds that produces a soup symphony. She stops them and teaches them the proper way to eat.

We leave the dinner scene and find the Queen in her chambers waiting for the Huntsman to return with Snow White's heart. He presents the swine's heart, but the magic mirror tells the Queen that Snow White is safe with the dwarfs. The furious Queen concocts the poison comb and sets off for the dwarfs' cottage to murder Snow White.

Returning to the cottage, we find dinner finished and the dwarfs putting on an entertainment for Snow White. They sing, dance, play homemade musical instruments, and so forth. Snow White tells them about her prince in a wistful song, and teaches them a dance of the court.

Bedtime ends the entertainment. The dwarfs curtain off a corner for Snow White and put several of their beds together to make her one big one. The dwarfs curl up wherever they can. Before saying "goodnight," Snow White makes the dwarfs kneel while she says a prayer.

Next morning, the dwarfs leave for the mine, but in the woods they decide they will take a day off and make Snow White a bed. With the help of the birds and animals, they make the bed, mattress, and comforter from the materials at hand in the forest.

While the dwarfs are making the bed, the Queen, disguised as a plump, jolly peddler, arrives at the cottage. While combing the snarls out of Snow White's hair, she sticks the poison comb into the girl's scalp and runs off.

The dwarfs, having finished the bed, put it on their shoulders and march home to surprise Snow White. They find her apparently dead. One of them finally finds the comb in her head and she revives when it is removed. They warn her against admitting strangers in the future and suspect that the peddler was either the Queen in disguise or one of her agents.

The Queen returns to the palace and is furious when the magic mirror again tells her that her schemes have failed and that Snow White lives. She breaks the mirror and goes to her laboratory to concoct the poison apple. Her book of magic tells her that the poison apple never fails. It produces a sleeping-living death so that its victims are buried alive. She taunts the Prince with the horrid details of her murderous scheme and, changing herself into a hag-like apple peddler, again sets out for the dwarfs' cottage.

No sooner has she left than the Prince escapes from his dungeon and sets out after the Queen. The escape is contrived by the birds who lure the guard away from the cell door, pick the keys from his pocket, and open the cell door. The Prince fights his way out of the palace and, mounting his horse, dashes off in hopes of killing the Queen before she kills Snow White. He loses the Queen's trail and, not knowing where Snow White is, will search the forest and countryside in vain, for months to come.

The dwarfs are at the mine when the Queen arrives at the cottage of the dwarfs. The dwarfs don't understand the warnings [from the animals] for some time, but finally, one of them gets the idea, and they dash to the rescue, riding deer, swinging from tree to tree like monkeys and so forth.

Meanwhile, Snow White has fallen for the Queen's persuasive words concerning the magic qualities of the poisoned apple—one bite makes your wish come true. Snow White makes her wish (that her prince takes her away), bites the apple, and swoons.

Just as the Queen scurries off, the dwarfs arrive. Most of them set off after the Queen. The chase ends when the Queen goes over a precipice and is killed. The dwarfs return. Doc meets them at the door. Snow White is dead. They kneel and pray.

At this point, sub-titles will tell us of the Prince's long search for Snow White, and how, after many months, he hears of a Princess sleeping in a gold and crystal coffin, watched over by the seven dwarfs. The dwarfs and little animals are surrounding the coffin when the Prince comes into the scene. They refuse to let him approach the coffin, but when he breaks into a song of lamentation for his dead love, they fall back.

Earlier in the story, we have told the audience that only the kiss from one's beloved can revive the victim of the poison apple. The Prince kisses Snow White. She opens her eyes and sits up in the coffin. He takes her in his arms and carries her to his horse, as the dwarfs, animals, and all nature unite in an ecstasy of joy. Followed by the dwarfs' farewells, Snow White and her Prince ride off, and we see them going to a castle in the clouds, while the doves ring the wedding bells.

Appendix B

Composite of Final Draft Scripts

January 5–December 2, 1937

"Story Book Opening"

Sequence 1B, scenes 3A-10 (January 5, 1937) "Queen and Mirror Sequence"

Sequence 2A, scenes 1-32 (November 11, 1937) "Snow White and the Prince in the Garden"

      2B, scenes 1-8 (November 10, 1937) "Queen Orders Snow White's Death"

Sequence 3A, scenes 1-51 "Snow White and the Huntsman"

      3B, scenes 1-32 "Snow White Meets Animals"

      3C, scenes 1-26B "Snow White Discovers Dwarfs' House"

      3D, scenes 1-18A "Snow White and the Animals Clean House"

Sequence 4A, scenes 1-19 (November 11, 1937) "Dwarfs at Mine"

      4B, scenes 1-5 (November 11, 1937) "Dwarfs March Home from the Mine"

      4C, scenes 1-18 "Snow White Discovers Bedroom"

      4D, scenes 1-53B (July 17, 1937) "Spooks"

Sequence 5A, scenes A1-47 (November 16, 1937) "Bedroom"

      5B, scenes 1-21 (November 10, 1937) "Snow White Tells Dwarfs to Wash"

Sequence 6A, scenes 1-36 "Dwarfs at Tub Washing"

      6B, scenes 1-46 (February 4, 1937) "Soup"

Sequence 7A, scenes AA1-33 (November 9, 1937) "Queen Leaves Mirror; Prepares Disguise"

Sequence 8A, scenes 1-62 (November 15, 1937) "Entertainment"

      8B, scenes 1A-26 (November 15, 1937) "Story Telling"

      8C, scenes 6A-30 (November 15, 1937) "Going to Bed"

Sequence 9A, scenes 1-13 (November 15, 1937) "Witch at Cauldron; Prepares Apple"

Sequence 10A, scenes 1-28 (November 15, 1937) "Dwarfs Leave for Mine"

      10B, scenes 1-3 (November 15, 1937) "Queen on Way to Dwarfs' House"

Sequence 11A, scenes 1-23 (November 15 , 1937) "The Lodge Meeting"

      11B, scenes 1-22 (October 15, 1937) "Bed-Building"

Sequence 13A, scenes 1-28 (November 10, 1937) "Snow White Making Pies; Witch Enters House"

Sequence 14B, scenes 5-13 (November 9, 1937) "Dwarfs at Mine; Animals Warn Them"

      14C, scenes 1-4 (November 10, 1937) "Witch Urges Snow White to Make Wish"

      14E, scenes 1-12 (November 9, 1937) "Dwarfs Start for House to Rescue Snow White"

      14F, scenes 1-6 (November 10, 1937) "Snow White Starts Wish"

      14G, scenes 1-5 (November 8, 1937) "Dwarfs on Way to House"

      14H, scenes 1-4A (November 9, 1937) "Snow White Dies"

      14J, scenes 1-30 (November 9, 1937) "Dwarfs Chase the Queen"

Sequence 15A, scenes 1-8 (December 2, 1937) "Snow White Dead"

      15B, scenes 1-3 (December 2, 1937) "Titles"

Sequence 16A, scenes 1-19 (December 2, 1937) "Snow White in Coffin; Back to Life; Away with Prince"

Fade Out - "And They Lived Happily Ever After."

Snow White and the Seven Dwarfs

Walt Disney presents
Snow White and the Seven Dwarfs
Adapted from Grimm's Fairy Tales

Supervising Director
David Hand

Sequence Directors
Perce Pearce
Larry Morey
William Cottrell
Wilfred Jackson
Ben Sharpsteen

Story Adaptation
Ted Sears
Otto Englander
Earl Hurd
Dorothy Ann Blank
Richard Creedon
Dick Rickard
Merrill De Maris
Webb Smith

Supervising Animators
Hamilton Luske
Vladimir Tytla
Fred Moore
Norman Ferguson

Animators
Frank Thomas
Dick Lundy
Arthur Babbitt
Eric Larson
Milton Kahl
Robert Stokes
James Algar
Al Eugster
Cy Young
Joshua Meador
Ugo D'Orsi
George Rowley
Les Clark
Fred Spencer
Bill Roberts
Bernard Garbutt
Grim Natwick
Jack Campbell
Marvin Woodward
James Culhane
Stan Quackenbush
Ward Kimball
Wolfgang Reitherman
Robert Martsch

Character Designers
Albert Hurter
Joe Grant

Art Directors
Charles Philippi
Hugh Hennesy
Terrell Stapp
McLaren Stewart
Harold Miles
Tom Codrick
Gustaf Tenggren
Kenneth Anderson
Kendall O'Connor
Hazel Sewell

Backgrounds
Samuel Armstrong
Mique Nelson
Merle Cox
Claude Coats
Phil Dike
Ray Lockrem
Maurice Noble

Songs
Frank Churchill
Larry Morey

Music
Frank Churchill
Leigh Harline
Paul J. Smith

Voice Talents
Snow White
Adriana Caselotti

The Prince
Harry Stockwell

The Queen
Lucille LaVerne

The Magic Mirror
Moroni Olsen

Sneezy
Billy Gilbert

Sleepy and Grumpy
Pinto Colvig

Happy
Otis Harlan

Bashful
Scotty Mattraw

Doc
Roy Atwell

The Huntsman
Stuart Buchanan

Sequence 1B, Scene 3A
Master layout: graphite on off-white paper
This opening scene was described as a "fade in from a long shot" on the final draft
script of January 5, 1937. With the perfection of the multiplane camera later that year,
it became a multiplane shot heightening the illusion of penetrating into the scene.

*"Magic Mirror on the wall,
who is the fairest one of all?"*

REG TO
MIRROR

Sequence 1B, Scene 4
*Animation drawing: graphite
   heightened with red and green
   pencil on off-white wove paper*
Animator: Art Babbitt
Babbitt's animation drawing of
   the Queen was to be
   registered to Wolfgang
   Reitherman's drawing of the
   Magic Mirror.

"SNOW WHITE!"

Sequence 1B, Scene 10
*Animation drawing: graphite and red
  pencil on off-white wove paper*
Animator: Art Babbitt

Sequence 1B, Scene 10
*Cel: ink and gouache on trimmed
  celluloid mounted to post-production
  airbrushed background*

*Sequence 2A, Scene 1
Cel setup: ink and
gouache on trimmed
celluloid mounted to
post-production
airbrushed background*

Sequence 2A, Scene 17
Cel setup: ink and gouache on celluloid on production watercolor background

"We are standing by a wishing well."

Sequence 2A, Scene 18
*Cel setup: ink and gouache on celluloid on production watercolor
background with watercolor-on-paper overlay*

"I'm wishing."

*Sequence 2A, Scene 9
Cel setup: ink and gouache
on celluloid on production
watercolor background*

*Sequence 2A, Scene 12
Rough layout: graphite heightened
with blue and red pencil on off-white paper*

"*I have but one song...*"

*Sequence 2A, Scene 24
Animation drawing: graphite,
red and green pencil on
off-white wove paper
Animator: Grim Natwick*

Sequence 2A, Scene 29
Production background: watercolor on white paper

"...only for you."

*Sequence 2A, Scene 31
Animation drawing:
graphite over red pencil on
off-white wove paper
Animator: Grim Natwick*

Sequence 2A, Scene 28
Layout tracing with camera mechanics: graphite and red pencil on off-white wove paper

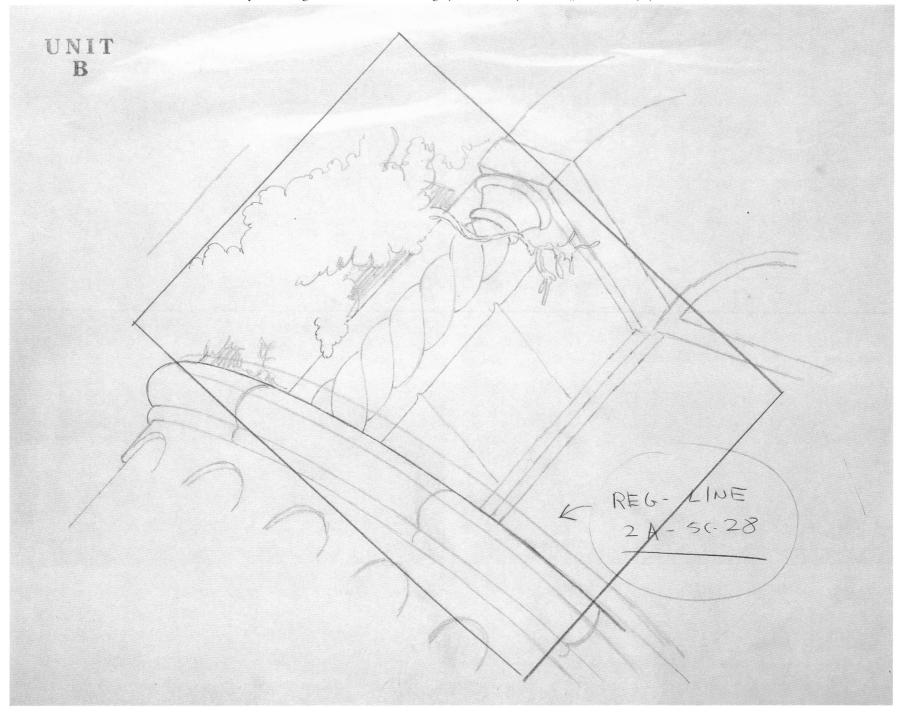

UNIT
B

REG - LINE
2A - SC. 28

"Bring back her heart in this!"

Sequence 2B, Scene 8
Cel: ink and gouache on
trimmed celluloid mounted
to post-production
airbrushed background

Sequence 2B, Scene 8
Cel: ink and gouache on
trimmed celluloid mounted
to post-production
airbrushed background

"Why? Why? I don't understand."

*Sequence 3A, Scene 2
Cel: ink and gouache
on trimmed celluloid*

Sequence 3A, Scene 9A
*Cel setup: ink and gouache on
  celluloid on production watercolor
  background with watercolor-on-paper overlay*
This background was also used for scenes 8, 8B, and 10.

"Run child! Run away! Hide! In the woods!"

Sequence 3A, Scene 17A
Cel setup: ink and gouache on celluloid on production watercolor background
This is the earliest production background in the Ison Collection. It was okayed for camera and stamped
"August 19, 1937," just four months before the premiere. The latest is stamped "November 18, 1937" (Sequence 3A, Scene 48).

Sequence 3A
Storyboard drawing: graphite
on off-white wove paper

Sequence 3A
Rough layout: charcoal and red pencil on buff wove paper
Art director: Gustaf Tenggren

Sequence 3A, Scene 49
Animation drawing: graphite
strengthened with red and blue
pencil on off-white wove paper
Animator: Jack Campbell

Sequence 3A, Scene 48
Special effects background: oil on white wove paper

"Please, don't run away."

Sequence 3B, Scene 7
*Animation drawing: graphite heightened with red
and green pencil on off-white wove paper*
Animator: Eric Larson
Larson's "scramming" animals were animated on one cel level, while Ham Luske's
Snow White, in their center, was animated on another.

"With a smile and a song."

Sequence 3B, Scene 14, no. 24
Animation drawing: graphite over
* red pencil on off-white wove paper*
Animator: Ham Luske

Sequence 3B, Scene 14, no. 33
Animation drawing: graphite over
red pencil on off-white wove paper
Animator: Ham Luske

"*Just like a doll's house.*"

Sequence 3C, Scene 2Bx
Rough layout: graphite on off-white paper

Sequence 3C, Scenes 2Ax–2Bx, and 3
Production pan background: watercolor on white paper

"Oh, it's dark inside."

Sequence 3C, Scene 2B
Cel setup: ink and gouache on celluloid on production watercolor background
To simulate Snow White wiping the window, John Hubley hand wiped each cel in this scene
when it was on the camera stand.

Sequence 3D, Scene 3A
Cel setup: ink and gouache on celluloid on production watercolor background

"Look at that broom!..."

Sequence 3C, Scene 13
Production pan background: watercolor on white paper
This background appeared on screen for three seconds in a pan
shot from left to a stop at right. The distorted drawing of the
stool and flagon simulated the visual effect of a quickly panning camera.

Sequence 3C, Scene 13
Layout tracing: graphite
on off-white paper

"...They've never swept this room."

Sequence 3C, Scene 13
Preliminary background: watercolor on white paper
Background artist: Arthur Fitzpatrick

"You do the dishes..."

Sequence 3C, Scenes 22, 24, and 26
Cel setup: ink and gouache on celluloid on production pan background in watercolor
Only a still shot of the right section (Scene 22) remained in the film.
The pan shots of Snow White sweeping in Scenes 24 and 26 were deleted,
according to the finalized draft script.

"...and I'll use the broom."

"If ya dig, dig, dig with a shovel or a pick in a mine, in a mine..."

Sequence 4A
Layout: graphite and ochre pencil on off-white paper

Sequence 4A, Scene 11
Cel: ink and gouache on celluloid

"...where a million diamonds shine."

Sequence 4A, Scene 3
Cel setup: ink and gouache on celluloid
on production watercolor background
Cel of Grumpy is key to this background, but the cel of Dopey is not.

Sequence 4A, Scene 10
Animation rough: graphite and ochre pencil on off-white wove paper
Animator: Fred Moore

"Heigh Ho, Heigh Ho..."

Sequence 4A, Scene 16
Production background: watercolor on white paper

"...it's home from work we go."

Sequence 4B, Scene 5
Preliminary background:
watercolor on white paper

"Door's open! Chimney's smokin'! Somethin's in there!"

Sequence 4D, Scene 16
Storyboard drawing with
camera mechanics:
graphite and red pencil
on off-white paper

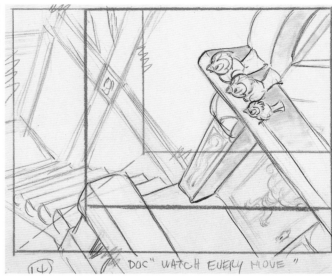

Sequence 4D, Scene 8
Cel setup: ink and gouache on trimmed celluloid on preliminary watercolor background

"It's up there. In the bedroom."

Sequence 5A, Scene A1
Production background: watercolor on white paper

"Jimminy crickets! What a monster!"

Sequence 5A, Scene 2
Layout: graphite on off-white paper

"Why, they're little men!"

*Sequence 5A
Cel: ink and gouache on celluloid*

*Sequence 5A
Cel: ink and gouache on celluloid*

*Sequence 5A
Cel: ink and gouache
on celluloid*

"Why wash? What for?"

Sequence 5B, Scene 6B
Cel setup: ink and gouache on celluloid on production watercolor background

"We ain't goin' nowhere."

Sequence 5B, Scene 13B
Animation drawing: graphite over
red pencil on off-white wove paper
Animator: Frank Thomas

Sequence 5B, Scenes 13–13B and Sequence 5A, Scenes 38E, 41A, and 43A
Cel setup: ink and gouache on trimmed celluloid on
production pan background in watercolor
The cels are not key to the background, which was painted for the fight between
Doc and Grumpy (Sequence 5A, Scenes 36–46), but was cut late in production.

"So splash all you like."

Sequence 6A, Scene 12
Cel setup: ink and gouache on celluloid on production watercolor background

Sequence 6A, Scene 16A
Animation drawing: graphite over
red pencil on off-white wove paper
Animator: Vladimir Tytla

"Get him over to the tub!"

Sequence 6A, Scene 24, no. 5
Animation drawing: graphite over red pencil on off-white wove paper
Animator: Vladimir Tytla

104

Sequence 6A, Scene 24, no. 9
Animation drawing: graphite over red pencil on off-white wove paper
Animator: Vladimir Tytla

"Get the soap!"

Sequence 6A, Scene 24A
Cel setup: ink and gouache on celluloid on production pan background in watercolor

Sequence 6A, Scene 24A, no. 21
Animation rough: graphite over red
pencil on off-white wove paper
Animator: Vladimir Tytla

Sequence 6A, Scene 24A, no. 21
Animation clean-up with color notations:
graphite with red and green
pencil on off-white wove paper
Animator: Vladimir Tytla
Color notations were added by the
Ink and Paint Department with reference
to the 1,500 numbered tints created
for the feature in Disney's Paint Lab.

"I've been tricked!"

Sequence 7A, Scene 4
Cel setup: ink and gouache on celluloid on production watercolor background

Sequence 7A, Scene 5
Animation drawing: graphite and
  red pencil on off-white wove paper
Animator: Robert Stokes

Sequence 7A, Scene 5
Trial cel (repainted): ink
and gouache on celluloid

"I'll go myself to the dwarfs' cottage in a
disguise so complete no one will ever suspect."

Sequence 7A, Scene 9
Cel setup: ink and gouache on celluloid on production pan background in watercolor

"Now a formula to transform my beauty into ugliness."

*Sequence 7A, Scene 9B
Cel: ink and gouache
on celluloid*

*Sequence 7A, Scene 21
Cel with lighting effect:
ink and gouache on celluloid*

Sequence 7A, Scene 21
Animation drawing: graphite over red pencil on off-white wove paper
Animator: Art Babbitt

"To age my voice, an old hag's cackle."

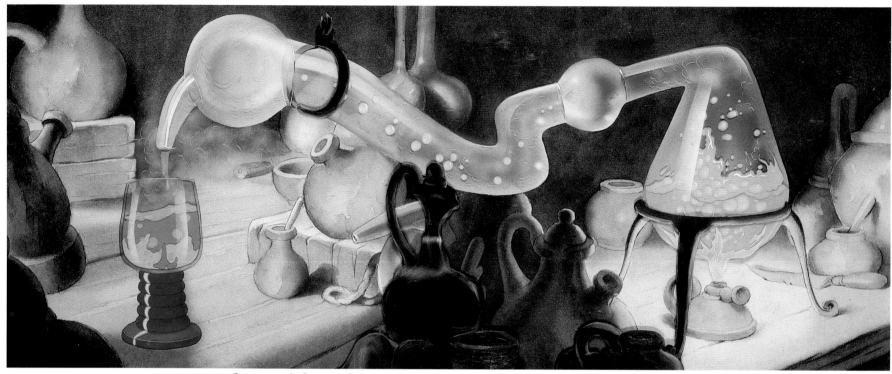

Sequence 7A, Scene 11C
Cel setup: ink and gouache on celluloid on production pan background in watercolor

"To whiten my hair, a scream of fright."

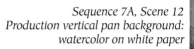

*Sequence 7A, Scene 12
Production vertical pan background:
watercolor on white paper*

*Sequence 7A, Scene 11C
Layout with camera mechanics:
graphite and red pencil on off-white
wove paper*

"And now a special sort of death for one so fair..."

Sequence 7A, Scene 19
Cel setup: ink and gouache on celluloid
on production watercolor background

"...What shall it be? Ah! A poison apple."

Sequence 7A, Scenes 31 and 31B
Cel setup: ink and gouache on celluloid on production watercolor background

Sequence 8A, Scene 13
Cel setup: ink and gouache on celluloid on production watercolor background

Sequence 8A, Scene 13
Rough layout: ochre pencil
strengthened with graphite
and red pencil on off-white
wove paper

Sequence 8A, Scene 24
Rough layout: ochre pencil
strengthened with graphite
and red pencil on off-white
wove paper

"Some day my prince will come."

Sequence 8B, Scene 10, no. 41
Animation rough: red pencil
  on off-white wove paper
Animator: Grim Natwick

Sequence 8B, Scene 10, no. 61
Animation rough: red pencil
  strengthened with graphite
  on off-white wove paper
Animator: Grim Natwick

Sequence 8B, Scene 10, no. 77
Animation rough: red pencil
strengthened with graphite
on off-white wove paper
Animator: Grim Natwick

"You're sure you'll be comfortable? Well, pleasant dreams."

Sequence 8C, Scenes 18 and 20
Production background: watercolor on white paper

"A fine kettle of fish!"

Sequence 8C, Scene 18
Animation drawing: red pencil
strengthened with graphite on
off-white wove paper
Animator: Grim Natwick

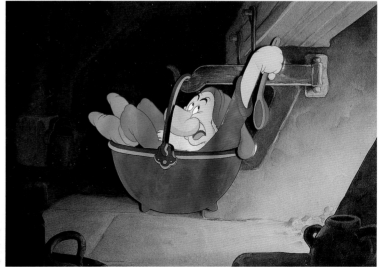

Sequence 8C, Scene 24
Cel setup: ink and gouache on celluloid
on production watercolor background
with watercolor-on-celluloid overlay

"Dip the apple in the brew..."

Sequence 9A
Cel: ink and gouache on trimmed
celluloid mounted to post-production
airbrushed background

"...Let the Sleeping Death seep through."

Sequence 9A
Cel: ink and gouache on trimmed celluloid mounted to post-production airbrushed background

"The little men will be away, and she'll be all alone."

Sequence 10B, Scene 1
Cel setup: ink and gouache on celluloid on production pan background in watercolor

Sequence 10B, Scene 3
Rough layout: graphite and
red pencil on off-white wove paper

Sequence 13A, Scene 6
Cel: ink and gouache on trimmed celluloid

Sequence 13A, Scene 5
Preliminary background:
watercolor on white paper

Sequence 13A, Scene 5
Production background:
watercolor on white paper
The word "flour" on the bowl
was airbrushed out in anticipation
of foreign language releases
of the film.

Sequence 13A, Scene 4
Production background: watercolor on white paper

"Mmmm. Makin' pies?"

Sequence 13A, Scene 13, no. 60
Animation drawing: graphite and red pencil with green pencil
 shadow indications on off-white wove paper
Animator: Norm Ferguson
These drawings were later autographed by Joe Grant,
the character model designer of the Witch.

Sequence 13A, Scene 13, no. 106
Animation drawing: graphite and
red pencil with green pencil
shadow indications on off-white
wove paper
Animator: Norm Ferguson

"Shame on you for frightening a poor old lady."

Sequence 13A, Scene 18
Layout drawing: graphite and red pencil on off-white wove paper
Scene 18 was deleted from this sequence.

Sequence 13A, Scene 22A
Production background: watercolor on white paper
Cels of the birds are from Sequence 3B and are therefore not key to this background.

Sequence 14B, Scenes 7A–7B and 8
Cel setup: ink and gouache on celluloid on production pan background in watercolor

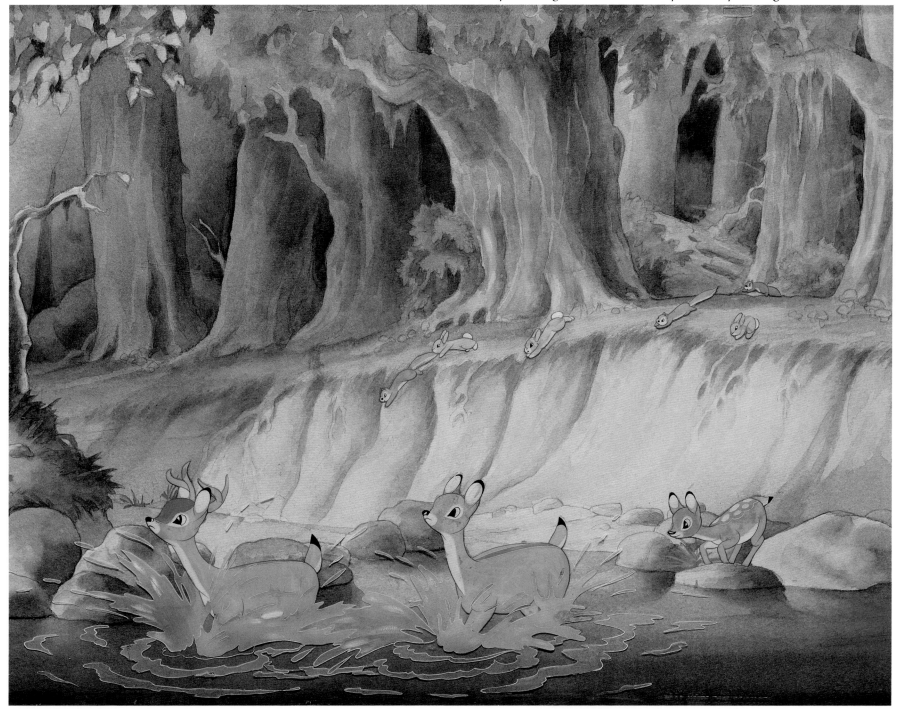

Sequence 14B, Scene 6
Cel setup: ink and gouache on celluloid on production pan background in watercolor

"Now take the apple, dearie, and make a wish."

SEQ. SCENE

14F   2

Sequence 14F, Scene 2
Animation drawing: graphite over red
pencil on off-white wove paper
Animator: Robert Stokes

Sequence 14F, Scene 3
Cel: ink and gouache
on trimmed celluloid

"*I wish...*"

Sequence 14H, Scene 1
Cel: ink and gouache on trimmed celluloid

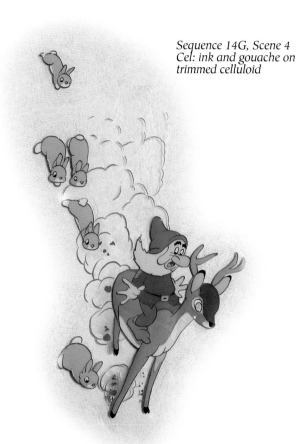

Sequence 14G, Scene 4
Cel: ink and gouache on
trimmed celluloid

Sequence 14G, Scene 5
Cel setup: ink and gouache on celluloid
on production pan background in watercolor

"I'm trapped!"

Sequence 14J, Scenes 22–27A
Layout inspiration sketches: charcoal heightened
with white on off-white paper
Art director: Kendall O'Connor

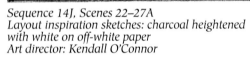

Sequence 14J, Scenes 22–27A
Layout inspiration sketches: charcoal heightened
with white on off-white paper
Art director: Kendall O'Connor

Sequence 14J, Scenes 22–27A
Layout inspiration sketches: charcoal heightened
with white on off-white paper
Art director: Kendall O'Connor

Sequence 14J, Scene 28
Cel: ink and gouache on trimmed
celluloid mounted to post-
production airbrushed background

Sequence 14J, Scene 29
Cel: ink and gouache on trimmed celluloid
mounted to post-production airbrushed background

The Sleeping Death

Sequence 15A, Scene 8
Animation drawing: graphite, red and blue pencil on off-white wove paper
Animator: Milt Kahl

144

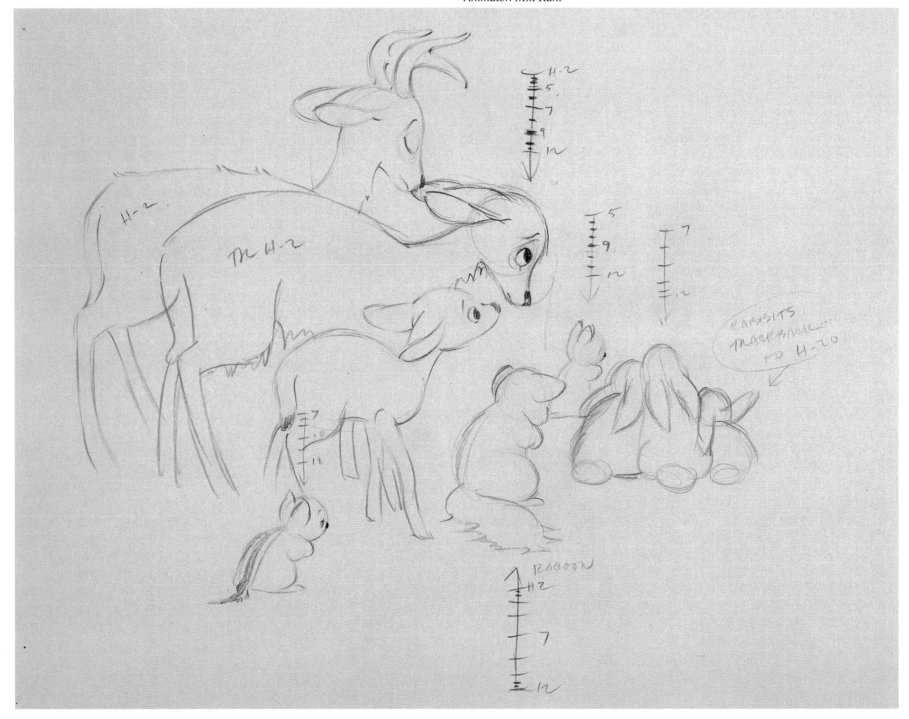

The Prince's Kiss

Sequence 16A, Scene 5, nos. 30 and 63
Animation drawings: graphite strengthened with
red and green pencil on off-white wove paper
Animator: Grim Natwick

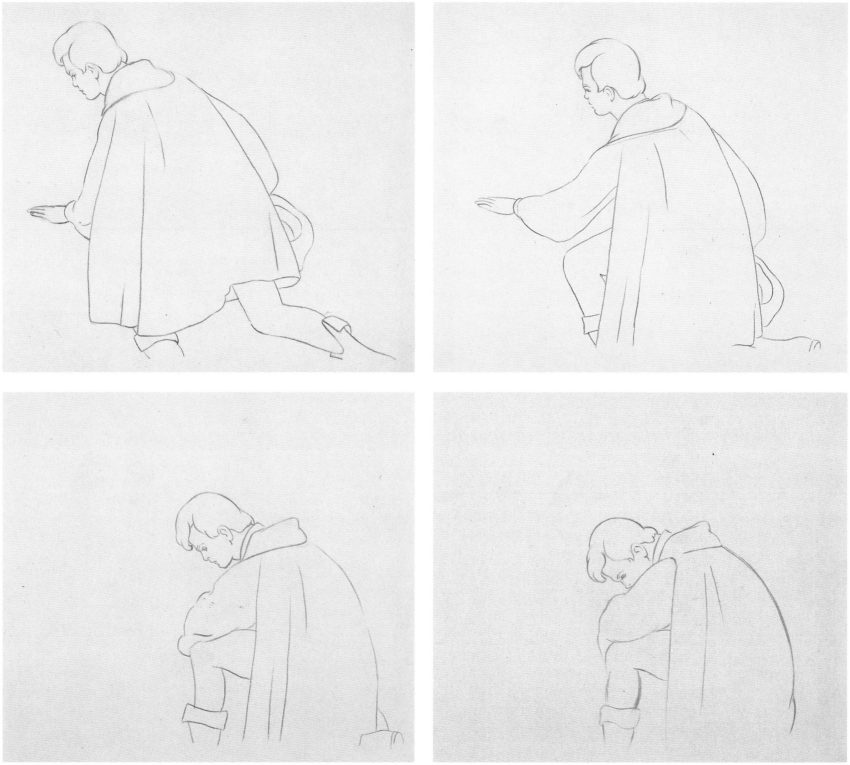

Sequence 16A, Scene 6, nos. 4, 14, 33, and 37
Animation clean-ups: graphite and red pencil on off-white wove paper
Animator: Grim Natwick

Sequence 16A, Scene 11A, nos. 8, 14, 24, and 34
Animation clean-ups: red pencil on off-white wove paper
Animator: Grim Natwick

Sequence 16A, Scene 13
Cel: ink and gouache on celluloid

"And they lived happily ever after."

Sequence 16A, Scene 15
Cel: ink and gouache on celluloid

Animation Art:
Its Production, Preparation for Sale, and Conservation

The Animation Process

Many of the principles and procedures of animation known today were developed for and utilized in the creation of Walt Disney's *Snow White and the Seven Dwarfs* sixty years ago. This is particularly true of the means by which the animated character was first conceived through story sketches and came to life, via animation drawings and painted celluloids ("cels"), on the film, complete with dialogue, music, and sound effects. It is difficult to imagine that each frame of film—twenty-four frames per second of running film for the eighty-three minutes of this animated feature—required the coordinated efforts of a minimum of eight artists: storyman, layout artist, background painter, animator, assistant animator, inker, painter, and cameraman. Accomplished without the aid of today's computers, instant color graphics, and video playback, all of these processes were done by hand and with the basic materials available at that time. The following discussion outlines the animation process and the materials used, from the animator's first sketches to the final cel setups, within the Disney studio during the creation of *Snow White and the Seven Dwarfs*.

By mid-1936 many months of work had already been spent on the full-length animated feature. Out of the initial planning meetings of 1934 and 1935 came a full script, from which individual story sketches were created, changed, expanded or deleted and then incorporated into a rough working order that showed the entire feature. The story sketches were organized and labeled into sixteen sequences, each of which contained several scenes. Phrases from the dialogue were written on the story sketches in comic strip fashion, along with any initial notes on action or mood. By timing a verbal reading of the dialogue of each scene and photographing the story sketches in their still form, it was possible to create a timed, filmed version of each scene. Splicing together all the filmed scenes in their proper order enabled the director to have an early idea of the sequence of events and the total length of the feature, even though nothing had yet been animated. This story reel soon became the working reel, as it would undergo several revisions before the film was completed.

In conjunction with this working reel, the studio made a soundtrack with the dialogue as it would actually be heard in the final film. Knowing the exact timing for each word and the spacing between words, a soundtrack reader could break the dialogue into the exact fraction of seconds required for each syllable and for the silent spaces between them. He then divided the timed dialogue into specific frames of film, according to the standard rate of twenty-four frames per second, and then recorded the information on exposure sheets (fig. 1). These sheets became the backbone of the film. For the remainder of production, all changes had to be noted on the exposure sheets as, ultimately, the cameraman followed all the instructions written on them.

As soon as the director approved a particular scene for animation, the animator received a record of the soundtrack, model sheets, a copy of the story sketches, a full scene description, and the exposure sheets for that scene. He also received a rough layout drawing of the scene indicating the character's size and action in relationship to the surroundings. The scale of the drawing—either "12 field," meaning a camera viewing area of 8¾ by 12 inches, or "16 field," with a camera viewing area of 11½ by 16 inches—was already determined by the director and layout artist. This rough layout was usually drawn with pencil on paper of the same size and type as the animator would use. If the animator had to animate one of the human characters—the Witch, Prince, Queen, Huntsman, or Snow White—he was also provided with a

Publicity cel

stack of rotoscope tracings for that scene.[1] These tracings resulted from filming a live actor or actress in costume acting out a particular scene and then putting the film into a rotoscope, a machine that projected the film onto a drawing board one frame at a time. An artist traced in registration onto a piece of animation paper the movement of the figure in each frame of film. Although these tracings were intended as guides for the lifelike movements of the human characters in *Snow White,* some animators found little use for them (fig. 2).

After reviewing all this material, the animator drew thumbnail sketches to work out the character action throughout the scene. From these sketches and the rough layout drawing, the animator then calculated the character action as it occurred across the scene into specific frames of film. Quite often he had further questions or suggestions for that scene and went back to confer with the director. Sometimes this would result in a change, such as alterations of the elements within the layout to achieve better character action. If this change affected the number of frames of film in any way (for example, adding frames to provide more time for a character to act), it was accurately noted on the exposure sheets for that scene. With everything finalized—for now—the scene was ready for animation.

The animator's drawing table contained a centrally located circular metal disk that was slightly higher than the surrounding wooden table.

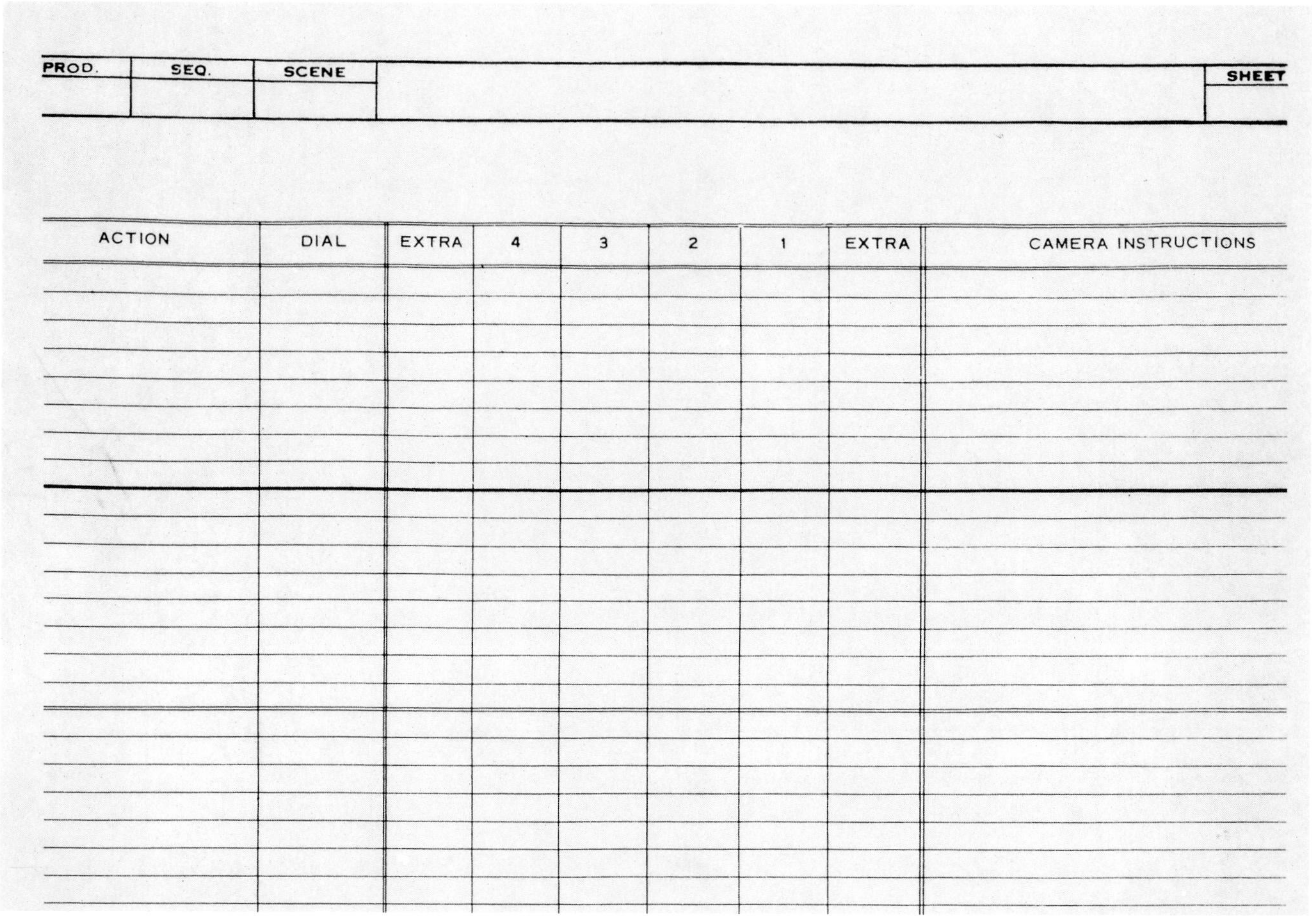

PROD.	SEQ.	SCENE		SHEET

ACTION	DIAL	EXTRA	4	3	2	1	EXTRA	CAMERA INSTRUCTIONS

Figure 1
Detail of an exposure sheet of the type used during the production of Snow White

Figure 2
Rotoscope tracing of Snow White

This animation disk freely rotated 360 degrees and was equipped with top and bottom peg bars configured as a two-prong/three-peg system. The drawing area within the disk was fitted with a piece of frosted glass that was lighted from behind. This system created a light box that enabled the animator to see through several drawings at a time while working. The drawing materials on the animator's table consisted of erasers, a pencil sharpener, a large amount of sharpened graphite pencils, any number of color pencils, and, most importantly, a stack of animation paper of the appropriate field size for that scene. Animation paper for a 12 field was 10 by 12 inches and for a 16 field 12½ by 15½ inches. The animation paper used at that time was a 24 lb. heavy weight, machine-made wood pulp paper from which lignin was removed during the sulphite wood pulping process. The pulp was also bleached for brightness. This paper carried the watermark (fig.3)

MANAGEMENT BOND
A HAMMERMILL PRODUCT

Originally produced by the Hammermill Paper Company (now International Papers) in Erie, Pennsylvania, this paper was considered the highest quality bond paper of its kind.[2] The studio then punched holes horizontally along one margin of the paper to fit the peg-bar system on the animator's disk. This peg system not only kept the character drawings registered to each other and to the layout drawing, but also provided the registration for the cels that would eventually be traced from them. The animator usually worked with the peg-hole registration along the bottom of the paper, as it allowed him to quickly review up to five drawings at one time.

Rough Animation

The animator worked through each scene, beginning to end, via a series of drawings in very rough form. Using the rough layout of the scene as a guide for the size and perspective of the characters, he drew only the most important points of a character's action. These were known as extremes. The animator numbered these animation roughs in the bottom right corner with the number indicating its order in the scene. If there were several characters animated within that scene, he put the letter A, B, C, or D next to the number. With A representing the bottom layer, these letters indicated the sequence in which drawings (and eventually the painted cels) containing simultaneous actions would be placed on top of one another for each frame of film. This information was also noted on the exposure sheet. In addition, the animator created spacing charts ("ladders" or "railroads") to indicate the number and spacing of the drawings that were to go between his extremes. He usually wrote the spacing charts in the lower righthand portion of the animation paper, though they were sometimes placed in other locations on the paper depending on the number of characters in and the complexity of the drawing (fig. 4).

Figure 3
Hammermill Paper Company watermark

Figure 4
Spacing charts on animation drawing

Figure 5
Animation drawing with
self-ink lines and color notations

At various times during the rough pencil animation of a scene, the animator may have had his day's work sequentially photographed on film so that he could view it in motion on the moviola, a projection box of Disney's design. Known as a pencil test, this film footage appeared in its negative form (that is, white pencil lines against a black background) because that was quicker and saved on printing costs. From this pencil test the animator determined if there should be any corrections in character action. If necessary, he made those changes before further work was put into the scene.

When a scene was finally completed in rough form, it was again photographed. The animator, among others, then viewed the pencil test of the rough animation, depicting mostly body action and gestures, with a recording of the dialogue and scrutinized it for synchronization between the body action and the words. Often he readjusted a scene, or portions of a scene, by one or more frames to achieve better character action in relation to the dialogue. Only then were the mouth movements for the dialogue added to the drawings in rough form.

It was not uncommon for a scene to go through several pencil tests during rough animation. Though the animator usually viewed his dailies on the moviola, longer portions of a pencil test were viewed in a small projection room known as "the sweatbox." It was here that Walt Disney, the director, layout artist,

and many of the animators critiqued the pencil tests. Only when all the main elements of a scene worked together in the pencil test were the drawings okayed for clean-up.

Clean-up Animation
Clean-up animation entailed tracing each rough animation drawing onto a new piece of Hammermill Management Bond paper with a smooth, clean line. This was the task of the assistant animator, who used the final layout for the background to accurately register the clean-up drawings he created from the animator's rough extremes. The character from an animator's rough was often barely discernible, so creating the clean-up drawing required a greater understanding of form, character action, and drafting skills than merely tracing a character outline. In addition, the assistant animator drew many of the drawings for movement that occurred between the animator's extremes (known as inbetweens); and for pan scenes he marked, along the bottom margin of the final layout for the background, the start and stop positions that the cameraman would follow.

To create the clean-up drawing, the assistant animator usually outlined the character with graphite, though often he first made a very light underdrawing in graphite or red color pencil.[3] Where necessary (the clothing, cheeks, noses, and beards of the dwarfs, for example), he also added the color separation lines ("self-ink lines" or "self-lines"), usually in red or green color pencil. The self-ink lines indicated that different colors were to be used in that area when the character was inked onto a cel. At this stage the

The Animation Process from the Animator's "Roughs" to the Cel Setup

Reconstruction by Linda Witkowski, with permission from The Walt Disney Company

Background: initial line tracing

Background: watercolor rendering

Animator's "rough" drawing

Clean-up drawing

Inked cel

Painted cel

Animator's "rough" drawing

Clean-up drawing

Inked cel

Painted cel

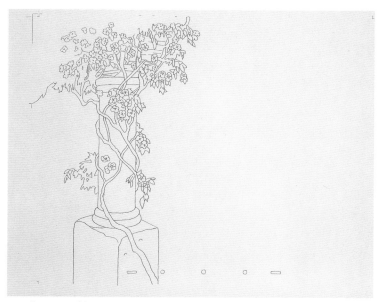

Overlay: initial line tracing

Overlay: watercolor rendering

Painted cel with black shadow cel

Painted cel with added special effects

Cel setup

assistant animator also added the character's shadow (fig. 5). (Animators in the Special Effects Department later added more extensive shadows and special effects on separate sheets of animation paper.) He then recopied the drawing number and, where applicable, drawing level and spacing charts onto the clean-up drawing. Other notations he may have indicated on the clean-up drawings include: (1) arrows and lines indicating where to register the character to the background; (2) instructions for how a character's head, body, or arm may arc when in movement; (3) color indicators, in the form of "X" or "𝓁" notations drawn with different color pencils, to denote shadows or the difference between the inside or outside of a character's clothing; and (4) notations to trace part of a figure from a previous drawing. A notation such as "TR. BAL. #21" abbreviates "Trace the balance of the figure from drawing number 21" (fig. 6). The assistant animator may also have put his initials in the bottom right corner of the drawing.

The few remaining drawings required for a scene were then drawn by the inbetweener, who proceeded in the same manner as the assistant animator. Added to the drawings were many of the notations discussed above, the corresponding drawing number, and, sometimes, the initials of the inbetweener.

Depending on the number and complexity of the character actions within a scene, each animator had one or more assistant animators, who worked with him in a private room. In contrast, all the studio's inbetweeners worked in a single large room (nicknamed the bullpen), and it was common practice for them to work for more than one animator at a time.[4]

The completed clean-ups for a scene may then have gone to the Special Effects Department, where animators added such elements as splashes of water, fire, rain, and teardrops to coincide with the character action. Special effects of this type were usually drawn on separate sheets of animation paper, which were numbered and lettered for drawing level to correspond to the matching character drawings.

At this point the cleaned-up drawings of a scene were checked again via a pencil test set against the final layout of the background. When the director and the layout artist established that the animated characters, special effects, and layout for a scene worked together properly, they okayed the animation drawings and final background layout for color.

The assignment (or "setting") of color for each scene involved deciding the colors for each character in each scene and deciding the color of the background against which that character would act. During the production of *Snow White,* the selection and setting of the character colors occurred first.[5]

Figure 6
Detail of an animation drawing with a "trace balance" notation

Ink and Paint

By the mid-1930s the Disney studio had established the Ink and Paint Department to formulate and catalogue a wide range of character colors. Each color was indicated by a letter or number combination and recorded on a master chart. Artists in this department consulted the master chart to make initial color selections.

Color Model Cels

To finalize the character colors, artists in the Ink and Paint Department created a color model cel for each character by selecting one drawing of that character within a particular scene and inking and painting the image onto a cel sheet (fig. 7). This cel acted as a guide from which the director, layout artist, and background painter determined the best possible colors for that character in each scene. Once decided, a model drawing of that character on animation paper was marked with ink and color notations indicating the specific character colors and the areas where they were to go (refer to fig. 5). The colors for each character often varied from one scene to the next, which meant indicating the different colors on a separate character model drawing representative of each scene.

Color Calculation

Once a character's colors were determined, the next step was to calculate the appropriate saturation or hue for the character color, which depended upon the cel level on which the character's action was to occur. The colors had to counteract the increasing grayness as the cels were layered for filming. For example, if a character acted on cel level A (bottom level) in one scene and on cel level D (top level) in another, the character colors for cel level A were the standard lighter and brighter colors, while in level D the colors were three tints ("let-downs") darker and grayer. This adjustment was necessary for the character's colors to appear the same in both scenes. Thus, once a character's colors were finalized for the bottom cel level, the Ink and Paint artists created at least three "let-downs" for each character color. Also, though used more extensively in other Disney features after *Snow White*, they sometimes created different sets of character colors for a character appearing in a daytime scene, a night scene, or in shadow.

Using the final color model cel for each character in conjunction with the additional color calculations (let-downs), artists in the Ink and Paint Department transferred the hundreds of animation drawings for each scene to clear celluloid sheets. This process involved (1) inking the character outline on the front of the cel; (2) painting the character color on the back of the inked cel; and (3) applying some special color effects to the front of the inked and painted cel.

Character Paints

Given that the smooth-surfaced cel sheet was the eventual support for the painted character, the paints needed special components to help them readily adhere as a uniform layer to the cel. Early experiments with such items as poster colors resulted in the paint film beading up on the cel and/or cracking away from the cel before it was photographed. The exact formulas used in the character paints remain studio secrets to this day. Nonetheless, it is possible to discern a few characteristics of the materials used in the paints for *Snow White*.

For example, because those paints were (and still are) soluble in water, they obviously contained some proportion of water mixed with powdered pigments. The pigments provided the basis for character color and must have been finely ground for overall uniformity. The general adhesion properties of the paint layer to the cel suggest that a water-based medium (such as gum arabic) was added as the binding agent. The resulting leveled surface of the colors indicates some smoothness and flexibility in the application of the paint. To achieve this, the addition of glucose, acting as a plasticizer, was necessary. To improve the brushability of the paints and increase the moistness of the colors, some proportion of glycerin had to be included in the mixture. The glycerin would also reduce any excessive caking and/or drying of the paints. It is important to note that the water-based paints did not bead up on the glasslike surface of the cel, which means that a wetting agent, such as oxgall or its equivalent, was added to the colors. Finally, to prevent mold growth in the paints and improve the odor of the colors, a preservative such as oil of cloves or formaldehyde would also have been added.

Character Inks

Among its other "firsts" as a full-length animated feature, *Snow White* pioneered the use of several different colors, rather than black ink, to outline a character. Basically, the color inks were derived by adding gray to a slightly darker version of a given character color and then thinning the mixture with water to the consistency of an ink.

Inking

In the months preceding the scheduled premiere of *Snow White* in December 1937, artists in the Ink and Paint Department went into full gear to complete the approximately 250,000 cels necessary for the feature.[6] A Disney memo of October 15, 1938, reveals that at one point the department employed 66 inkers, each inking approximately 28 cels per eight-hour day, while 178 painters each completed

approximately 21 cels per eight-hour day.[7] The task of inking the character outline was usually done by women, because experience had proven that they could do the job with a higher degree of neatness and consistency than their male counterparts. High-quality drafting skills, exacting fluidity, and neatness were essential, especially since, in the final projected film, the character outlines were magnified many times on the movie screen.

The transparent celluloid sheets used for *Snow White* were .005 millimeters thick and composed of cellulose nitrate. The cel was registered along the bottom with the same peg-hole system as the animation paper. The most important factors in inking a cel were (1) obtaining a smooth, opaque character outline; (2) accuracy and fluidity when tracing the character outline from the clean-up animation drawing, especially when the registered line was made, as it had to align with the background or another cel, and when trace-backs were concerned, as there would be no movement on the screen in those areas (for example, the feet of a character); and (3) accuracy in closing off all areas of a character outline, so that, for example, a character's tongue, his teeth, and mouth opening were clearly separated and thus able to completely contain the character colors. In addition, when a portion of a character extended beyond the viewing range, or field, of the camera, a field line indicating the parameters of the character colors in that area was drawn near the sides,

Figure 7
Color model cel

Figure 8
Detail of applied character special effects

top, or bottom of a cel. The field line was never visible in the final film.[8]

Wearing white cotton gloves to keep both sides of the cel free from scratches, fingerprints, oil, and grease, inkers applied the character outline to the front of the cel by tracing over each of the cleaned-up drawings with an extremely fine crow quill pen nib loaded with the appropriate color. For example, the cel setup of Snow White at the wishing well used four different colors in her character outline and three different colors to outline the doves. Evenly applying the character inks to the slick surface of the cel was not easy, as a small speck of dust or lint on the cel or in the pen nib could result in an unexpected blob of color within the linear outline of a character. Finally, the corresponding drawing number and (if applicable) level were inked in the bottom right corner of the front of the cel.

Painting

Once dry, the inked cels were ready for the character colors. The most important factors in painting the cel were (1) applying the character colors smoothly and opaquely, especially on the cels that were to be placed on the individually lit levels of the multiplane camera for photographing; (2) remaining within the character outline; and (3) keeping the painted cels clean and unscratched, which meant wearing white cotton gloves. The painter also had to apply the colors accurately and with a great deal of speed.[9]

Working from painted model cels or character model drawings on paper that noted the particular colors for each character, the

painters, usually women, applied the colors to the back of the cel.[10] For light colors they thinned the paint with water to a creamy consistency and then floated it onto the cel with a brush. Many of the dark values, however, would lose their opacity if thinned to a creamy consistency, so they had to be directly brushed onto the cel in a slightly drier form.[11] The painters applied the darkest colors first, so that any overlap of colors would not be visible when the cel was placed face up. It could be a complex job, as, for example, the cel setup of Snow White at the wishing well called for eight different character colors for her and two different colors for the doves.

Special Effects:
Characters

After inking and painting a character, any special effects for the *character* (not the scene) were added to the front of the cel. For Snow White this included a highlight around her hair, created by applying a small amount of darker gray-brown character paint with a dry brush along the edges of her hair. Also, legend has it that her cheeks received a smudge of rouge because, in the first completed scenes, she looked too pale. Someone suggested literally putting rouge on her cheeks, but Disney questioned whether or not it could be applied evenly from cel to cel. The women in the Ink and Paint Department told him not to worry, because they had plenty of personal experience applying rouge! In the end, they put the blush in Snow White's cheeks with red

161

lipstick applied as dryly as possible with the tip of a finger.[12] This same technique was also used effectively on the Queen (fig. 8).

Special Effects:
Candlelight, Shadows

To emphasize a lit candle (as when Dopey walks upstairs to find the "monster" in the bedroom), the painters surrounded its flame with a warm, glowing haze. Using thinned-down character paints of the appropriate color, they applied the golden glow with an airbrush either on a separate blank cel or on the front of the inked and painted cel.

Any shadows cast by a character on the ground were painted with black paint onto a separate cel (fig. 9). The shadow cel was then photographed with the corresponding character cel at only a portion of the total exposure time for that scene. After backing up that segment of the partially exposed film, the cameraman rephotographed the scene without the shadow cels at the remaining exposure time. The double-exposed film yielded an evenly toned shadow.

In a similar manner, the painters created a black mask with a brush or, for a softer effect, an airbrush for those portions of a background or the body of a character (hat, face, arms, clothing, etc.) that moved into shadow. Along with the corresponding character cel, this type of shadow cel was photographed in the double-exposure manner previously described. These special shadow masks alleviated the need for devising a completely new set of character colors for the shaded portion of a scene.

Figure 9
Detail of a cel setup with added black shadow cel

Figure 10
Detail of a cel setup with added water special effects cel

162

Special Effects Department

More dynamic effects such as dust, smoke, rain, teardrops, lightning, water effects, and background depth required different approaches. By the time *Snow White* was in production, the Disney studio had its own Special Effects Department to handle these tasks.

Artists in this department added the rain, splashing water, teardrops, or smoke only after the character movement for the scene was animated in pencil and approved. Working with these character drawings, the special effects animators designed the effect to synchronize with the character's movements in a portion of a scene. They drew most of the special effects of this type on separate pieces of animation paper, numbered each, and assigned it a level (A, B, C, or D) corresponding to its character drawing, which also indicated whether it went on top of or underneath the character. In some cases the special effects animation was added directly to the character animation drawing.

Once completed, each drawing of special effects animation was inked and/or painted onto a cel (fig. 10). The materials and techniques for applying the ink and paint to many of the special effect cels were similar to those used in the inking and painting of the character cels. There were, however, many innovative approaches as well, such as using an airbrush to create the effect of dust or smoke. To create such realistic effects as the water ripples in Snow White's and the Prince's reflections in the wishing well, the artists painted a clear lacquer on the cel. The illusion of falling rain in other places resulted from combining a special effects animation of raindrops with actual film footage of falling rain.

Lightning effects utilized still another approach. Artists painted separate black and white silhouetted images corresponding to the appropriate painted character and production background. When this portion of the scene was photographed, the black and white silhouettes were alternated with each other, the color image, and the background. The result was a flashing effect that, when combined with a soundtrack, gave the lifelike illusion of character action within lightning. Adding rain on top of this gave the effect of a full thunderstorm.

Some scenes required subtle undulations in a body of water (such as a pond) or in portions of a background. Moving a piece of distressed or textured glass in a given direction during the photographing of each frame of film for that scene achieved the desired effect. It also gave that area a subtle but realistic feeling of added depth. In *Snow White* these types of effects are noticeable in some of the forest scenes where the animals are eating near the water and—combined with the special effects animation of smoke—in the scenes where the Magic Mirror responds to the Queen's inquiries.

Backgrounds

While a character was evolving from clean-up animation to the painted cel, the background artist began working on the production background for the scene. He first created a series of thumbnail color sketches that suggested the overall mood for the scene. While executing these sketches, he referred to the final layout drawing of the background and the corresponding color model cels of the characters. He, the director, and the layout artist then selected the color key for the scene from these sketches, after which he often created a preliminary background or color study of the background in the appropriate colors. Some were painted with Winsor & Newton watercolors on Strathmore medium-weight, cold-pressed, smooth-surface paper, though other types of paper were used as well.[13] The preliminary background usually served as the model from which the production background was painted (refer to p. 129).

The painted background used in production had to accurately correspond in scale to the final layout for a scene, as all the character and special effects animation was registered to it. The final layout also served as a guide to those areas that had to be empty so

that the elements within the background did not compete with the character action. For *Snow White* the production backgrounds were executed with Winsor & Newton watercolors on 90 lb. cold-pressed Whatman's watercolor paper that had a rough texture.[14] Prior to applying any paint to the watercolor paper, the background artist prepared it by thoroughly wetting it with water. He then blotted off the excess water and stretched the wet piece of paper by attaching it to a flat surface with gummed brown paper tape along each edge. Once dry, the paper remained flat, regardless of how many washes of watercolor the background artist applied.[15]

As many as 729 different backgrounds were required for *Snow White,* so the color schemes and overall tone had to be carefully planned and followed from background to background for there to be visual uniformity in the final film. After tracing each background composition from its corresponding final layout onto the prepared watercolor paper, the artist rendered the entire background with washes of Payne's gray watercolor, which helped achieve uniformity among the backgrounds.[16] During this process the artist indicated the darkest shadows and intermediary tones with some level of detail and left unpainted areas for the highlights. The result was a fairly

complete black-and-white rendering of the background. At this point the artist added the washes of different color. Some production backgrounds also received dark linear accents drawn in with graphite or gray-black watercolor. Cobwebs (as in the dwarfs' cottage) were the last touches on the production background, applied with a thin wash of permanent and/or Chinese white (fig. 11).

For some scenes the production background may have included overlays because the character action occurred behind certain elements, such as the left pillar in the foreground of Snow White's wishing well. The overlays were executed on separate pieces of watercolor paper with the same materials and techniques employed in the production backgrounds. Once completed, the overlay was carefully trimmed from the watercolor paper and attached to a clear sheet of celluloid the same dimensions as the production background.[17] A background artist worked in this manner on up to five backgrounds at one time,[18] which aided the visual continuity of color from background to background.

When the artist finished a group of backgrounds, he pinned them to a large panel in their appropriate sequence. The color model cel for each scene was placed over the

Figure 11
Detail of production background with painted cobwebs

background and the readability of the character was again checked against it. If the color relationships and mood within a scene worked, and worked as well with those scenes on either side of it, the completed rendering received final approval, signified by an inked authorization stamp usually placed on the back of the background. During the production of *Snow White*, the handwritten initials of Sam Armstrong, background supervisor, accompanied this inked stamp (fig. 12).

At this point, the peg-hole registration system was cut along the bottom of the background. Any notations for the cameraman, such as pan moves, supplied by the animator on the final layout for that scene were transferred to the bottom margin on the front of the production background in graphite (fig. 13). Additional information regarding the sequence, scene, number of cel levels, overlays, and special effects were also noted by hand with graphite in an inked, stamped area on the back of the background. Accompanying these notations were the initials or signature of Jack Atwood, head checker (refer to fig. 12). If all the elements of a scene worked correctly against the notations on the exposure sheet, the entire scene was ready to be photographed.

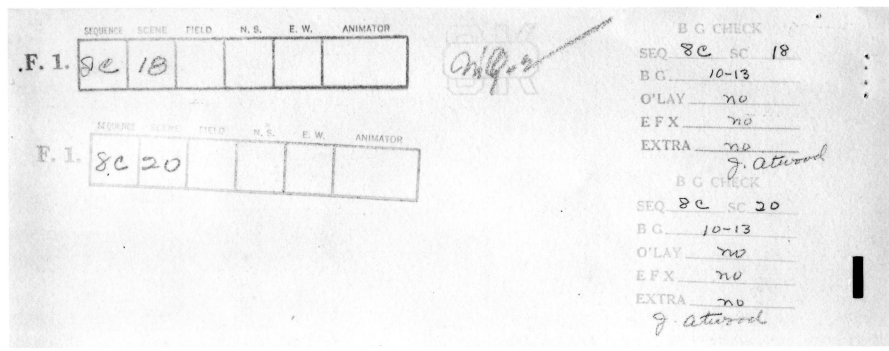

Figure 12
Authorization stamps on reverse of production background

Final Photography

When a scene was approved for photography, the cels, production backgrounds, and, most importantly, the exposure sheets were taken to the camera room. On them the various departments had recorded all the changes that occurred during the animation process, and the cameraman relied exclusively on these notations when photographing the hundreds of cels for each scene. Only by following this information could he accurately place the character cels in sequence and at the appropriate level, as well as place the shadow cels and special effects cels. This was essential if the character movement were to function properly and the color be consistent from one scene to the next.

Prior to production of *Snow White*, the studio had invented, tested, and implemented the multiplane camera, which had four to six levels stacked on top of one another, including the level carrying the camera. Each level was constructed of a heavy metal frame and a glass work surface that took four technicians to move. Each also contained the two-prong/three-hole peg-bar system that kept the artwork in accurate registration, was individually lit with up to eight 500-watt bulbs, and had its own exhaust vent to control the excessive heat of the lights. The camera was located at the top of the apparatus, while the work surface for the production background was usually at the bottom (fig. 14). Between them were layered the character movement cels and overlays. Photographing each character or portion of a scene at a different distance from the camera enhanced the illusion of depth, as in the opening scenes of the Queen's castle.

All the calculations for the camera—for trucking and/or pan shots and for the movements of each level—were done manually and required the talents of a skillful engineer.

Where the scene did not require the illusion of depth, the standard animation camera was utilized (refer to fig. 14). In this setup, the camera, located at the top of the vertical metal frame system, pointed straight down onto a single flat work surface containing the two-prong/three-hole peg-bar that kept the artwork registered. A large piece of glass, called a platen, placed over the background and the painted cels kept them flat during photography. An example of a scene photographed in this manner is Snow White and the doves at the wishing well.

With both the multiplane and standard animation camera systems, the cels for a cel setup (that is, the production background on top of which one to four layers of character and/or special effects cels were registered) had to be changed for each frame of film. Many scenes were rephotographed via double or triple (or more) exposure to create the final shadow and lighting effects in each scene.

Once the photography of a scene was completed, a final stamp was placed on the reverse of the production background and initialed by the cameraman. Each scene was then edited, the scenes were spliced together in the appropriate order, and the film was combined with a synchronized soundtrack, complete with music, dialogue, and sound effects. From this film several prints were made and shipped to theaters for audiences to enjoy.

From the initial story sketches to the production background and painted cels, over 2,500,000 pieces of art in some form were required to create the eighty-three minutes of *Snow White and the Seven Dwarfs*.[19] For those viewing *Snow White*, the results of the coordinated efforts of the storymen, layout and background artists, animators, assistant animators, inkers, painters, and cameramen speak for themselves.

Figure 13
Detail of pan move notations along bottom margin of production background

Figure 14
The camera room at Hyperion studio in 1937, with multiplane camera (left) and standard animation camera (right)

Figure 15
Airbrushed post-production background

Preparation of Animation Art for Sale

By 1938 the characters of Snow White and the dwarfs had grown in popularity. Increasing sales of *Snow White* merchandise plus the overtures of Guthrie Courvoisier, owner of a fine art gallery in San Francisco, convinced Walt and Roy Disney that the original artwork from the film should be made available for sale through art galleries worldwide. They selected only those works from *Snow White* that could hold up well when viewed as individual units. Most of the animation drawings were saved for the animators' future reference and are housed in the Disney Animation Research Library. Once photographed, many of the remaining cels were destroyed or washed for re-use.[20] During 1938 only selected painted cels from *Snow White* were released for sale. However, a March 7, 1939, listing of the artwork from *Snow White* eventually sold through Courvoisier Galleries consisted of 150 backgrounds, 206 story sketches, 500 animation drawings, and 8,136 celluloids.[21]

Initially the original animation art was matted and prepared for sale within the Disney studio. The selected story sketches, animation drawings, and some backgrounds were matted and framed, while the cels were cut down in size or individual characters were trimmed

from the cel sheet. The cel sheets were then taped or the trimmed characters were glued directly to one of the following types of backgrounds: (1) hand-painted watercolor production backgrounds that were used in the production of the film; (2) hand-painted watercolor preliminary backgrounds that closely resembled the production backgrounds in scale and overall color, though they did not have any authorization stamps on the back and were not used in the final film; and (3) simplified backgrounds that were created specifically for the sale of the cels. These simplified backgrounds were not used in the film in any way and were of three basic types: (1) simple water-based, airbrushed backgrounds on a thin piece of facing paper that merely suggested the elements of the original production background (fig. 15); (2) mounted wood veneer backgrounds, often containing airbrushed shadows and/or the name of the particular character (figs. 16a and 16b); and (3) backgrounds comprised of a piece of thin, patterned wrapping paper (fig. 17). These simplified background illustrations were then glued to cardboard.

For those cels that were trimmed and glued directly onto the background, a blank cel sheet was usually cut to the outer dimensions of the background, placed over the painted cel and background, and

taped along all edges with cellophane tape. When the characters were still part of the cel sheet, that sheet would be taped to the background, with or without a blank cel on top. In either case, the cel/background package was then taped to the back of a window mat board with cellophane or gummed paper tape. Often the name of the character would be written in graphite underneath the aperture of the window mat. During 1938 printed identification stickers were attached to the back of the background. They usually read: "This material inflammable. Handle with care. Frame under glass. Copyright 1937. Walt Disney Enterprises" and "Original work from *Snow White and the Seven Dwarfs*" (fig. 18).

By 1939 a different printed identification sticker was attached to the reverse of the background. For example, a production background from *Snow White* carried an identification sticker that read: "This original master 'background' and 'cel' painting from the Walt Disney Studios was used in the filming of *Snow White and the Seven Dwarfs*. Only one background is made for each scene, consequently this is the only one of its kind in existence. Copyright 1937. All rights reserved. Walt Disney Productions" (fig. 19). Below this heading, in smaller print, was a brief description of the

Figures 16a and 16b
Wood veneer post-production backgrounds

THE HUNTSMAN

animation process, followed by a listing of the museums that had purchased this animation art. This was the basic format of the label used by Courvoisier Galleries through 1946.

In the late 1930s Disney employed twenty people to prepare the animation art for the Courvoisier Galleries. From 1940 (after the release of artwork from *Pinocchio*) until September 1946 Courvoisier assumed responsibility for preparing the art for sale.[22] During this period, the backgrounds and method of cel preparation remained largely the same; however, another form of presenting the cel, via lamination, was added to the process.

Generally, the lamination process involved backing a painted character cel with an additional blank cel sheet. Sometimes the front of the character cel also had a blank cel sheet laminated to it. In other instances, two or more character cels from the same scene were laminated together and then backed with an additional blank cel sheet. A relatively clear, sticky glue was used as the adhesive. The purpose of the lamination process was to protect the water-soluble character outline and color from being damaged. The cels laminated in this manner were then cut down to the same size as the background with which they were framed. Cellophane tape and/or glue was used to attach a laminated cel to its corresponding background. The cel/background package was then taped to the back of the window mat with cellophane or gummed paper tape. As with the earlier cels sold through Courvoisier Galleries, the name of the character was often written with graphite just

Figure 17
Wrapping paper post-production background

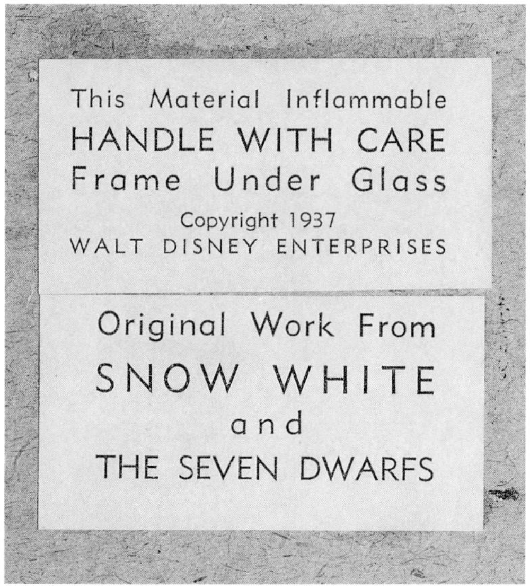

Figure 18
Courvoisier identification labels, 1938

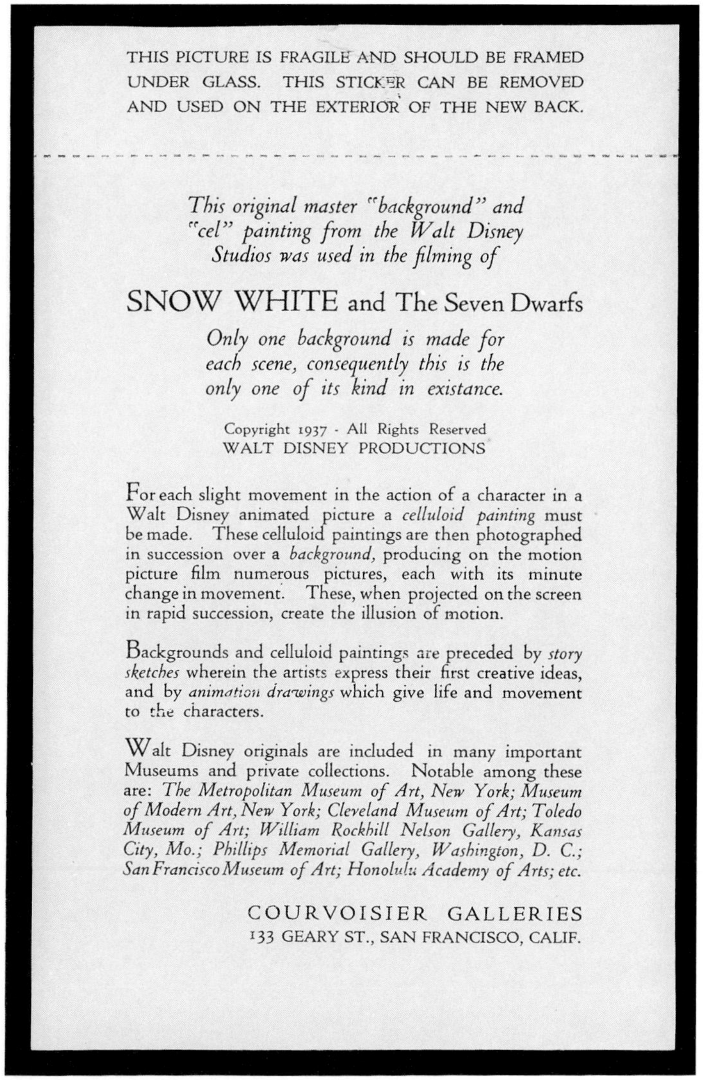

THIS PICTURE IS FRAGILE AND SHOULD BE FRAMED UNDER GLASS. THIS STICKER CAN BE REMOVED AND USED ON THE EXTERIOR OF THE NEW BACK.

This original master "background" and "cel" painting from the Walt Disney Studios was used in the filming of

SNOW WHITE and The Seven Dwarfs

Only one background is made for each scene, consequently this is the only one of its kind in existance.

Copyright 1937 - All Rights Reserved
WALT DISNEY PRODUCTIONS

For each slight movement in the action of a character in a Walt Disney animated picture a *celluloid painting* must be made. These celluloid paintings are then photographed in succession over a *background*, producing on the motion picture film numerous pictures, each with its minute change in movement. These, when projected on the screen in rapid succession, create the illusion of motion.

Backgrounds and celluloid paintings are preceded by *story sketches* wherein the artists express their first creative ideas, and by *animation drawings* which give life and movement to the characters.

Walt Disney originals are included in many important Museums and private collections. Notable among these are: *The Metropolitan Museum of Art, New York; Museum of Modern Art, New York; Cleveland Museum of Art; Toledo Museum of Art; William Rockhill Nelson Gallery, Kansas City, Mo.; Phillips Memorial Gallery, Washington, D. C.; San Francisco Museum of Art; Honolulu Academy of Arts; etc.*

COURVOISIER GALLERIES
133 GEARY ST., SAN FRANCISCO, CALIF.

Figure 19
Courvoisier identification label, 1939–46

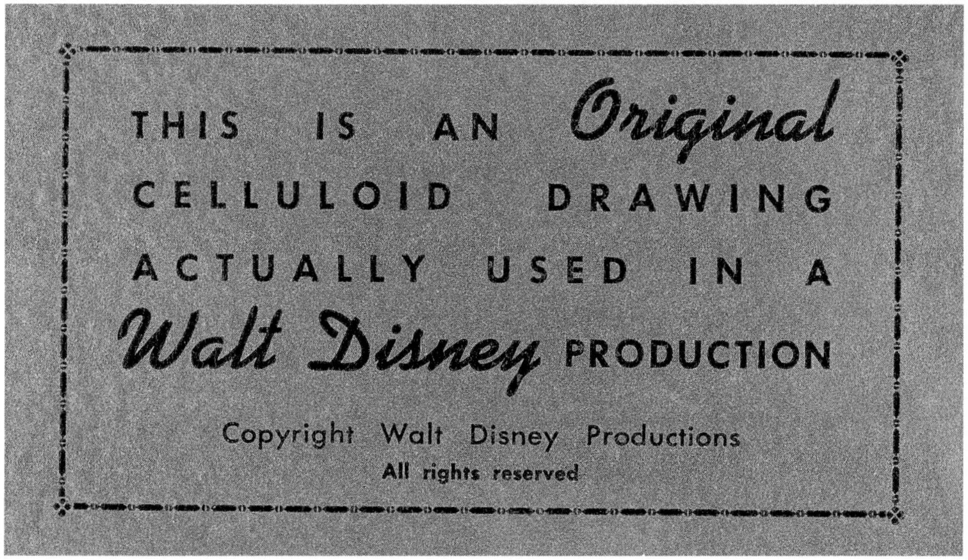

Figure 20
Art Corner identification label

below the aperture of the window mat. In addition, the monogram W_pD (Walt Disney Productions) was often stamped with ink on the background or the window mat, and the appropriate identification sticker was applied to the back.

Until September 1946 original Disney animation art was prepared and sold solely via Courvoisier Galleries. From 1946 until 1955 Walt Disney Productions periodically released hand-painted cels. When Disneyland opened in 1955, the marketing of original Disney art, beginning with the release of *Lady and the Tramp*, resumed on a regular basis in the Art Corner gift shop.[23]

For the most part, cels available in the gift shop were cut down to fit the dimensions of a piece of colored mat board that acted as a backing support. The painted cel sheet was stapled along the top and bottom to the backing board. This package was then taped to a thin window mat with masking tape or gummed paper tape. There was no inscription on the window mat, nor any Walt Disney Productions monogram. A sticker, however, was attached to the reverse of the backing board: "This is an original celluloid drawing actually used in a Walt Disney Production. Copyright Walt Disney Productions. All rights reserved" (fig. 20). Since the opening of Disneyland in 1955, the preparation and marketing of original Disney art has remained the responsibility of the Walt Disney Company.

Figure 21
Irregularities in a cel sheet

Conservation of Animation Art

When first marketed in 1938, the painted cels and backgrounds appeared similar to the actual film in coloration and richness. With the passage of time, however, the appearance of many of the painted cels and backgrounds—especially the production backgrounds—has changed. Where the cel sheets were originally quite flexible, clear, and flat, they have since become more brittle and (with cellulose nitrate cels) yellowed. Also there is often an irregular curling of the cel sheet within the painted character and/or along the taped edges of a cel sheet that has been cut down (fig. 21). The painted character outline, originally a nicely flowing, uniform line, now often exhibits areas of flake loss, scratches, and slight fading. Probably most affected by the passage of time are the painted character colors. Originally combinations of continuous areas of rich and muted colors (depending on the character), they now often exhibit variances of tonality because of: (1) fading due to excessive exposure to light; (2) uneven discoloration from lacquer, nail polish, rubber cement, or cellophane tape that was applied directly to the back of the character color; and (3) varying degrees of cracking, flake loss, and delamination resulting from unstable components in the paints and/or exposure to rapidly changing temperature and extremes in relative humidity.

Along similar lines, the preliminary and production backgrounds executed with watercolors originally contained many degrees of subtle colors. The colors in many of these backgrounds have now faded in varying degrees as a result of long-term exposure to light. Most noticeable is the decrease in the color intensity of the yellows, reds, dark blues, and blacks. The paper on which the backgrounds were created has also yellowed slightly over time. Fortunately, even with these changes, many of the backgrounds still retain their overall beauty and the continuity and balance of color tone.

Also affected by the passage of time are many of the simplified backgrounds that were prepared for those cels sold through the Courvoisier Galleries. The colors in many of these backgrounds have faded as a result of light exposure and, particularly with the simplified airbrushed backgrounds, there often appears an uneven dark red-brown staining throughout (fig. 22). This type of overall staining is often the result of the aging of the adhesive that was used to attach the facing paper to the cardboard support.

With the aging of the composite materials, many of the early animation cels and backgrounds now appear to have a yellow glow or patina. It is important to remember that this is part of the natural aging process of these materials. Interestingly, within each cel/background package this aging has occurred evenly, so that the painted cel and its background still appear in balance. This is true as well of the story sketches and animation drawings. The result of the aging process is that the early animation cels and backgrounds no longer appear exactly the same as the film, especially when compared to those animated films that recently have been digitally restored to their original appearance.

What should be done in the event of cracking, delamination, and/or flaking of the painted character colors? Some animation restorers completely wash off all the original character colors and repaint the entire character. Though this approach may save time, it robs the cel of its original paint layer. The restorers often make no written and/or photographic record of the aged original character colors before removing them; and in an attempt to recreate a character color as it may have initially appeared, the restorer's color matching can sometimes appear to be too rich or bright and not in balance with the aged cel sheet and/or corresponding background. When carried out to its fullest, this restorative approach obviously destroys the historic character of the cel. It is also likely to create a false balance of character coloration when one takes into account that the character colors from scene to scene and from cel level to cel level can often be very different. The aesthetic value of restoring a painted cel or preserving it in its current state should be carefully considered.

Early animation art was never created with longevity in mind, so the surviving vintage cels from *Snow White* exhibit natural yellowing of the cel material as well as some level of crackle or flake loss in the painted character. With this in mind, the collector of animation art should ensure care and handling that preserves its current appearance and longevity and establish a well-rounded conservation approach geared toward maintaining the artistic, historic, and structural integrity of animation art. This approach should not only limit the scope of the repairs to the animation art, but also focus on the many aspects necessary for its preservation.

Figure 22
Staining on a post-production airbrushed background

178

Preservation

Inhibiting the further deterioration or damage of animation art requires that environmental conditions such as temperature, relative humidity, light exposure, and atmospheric pollutants be carefully controlled (even if a collector's "museum" is his or her home). Preventive conservation also includes the design and use of archival materials within which animation art can be safely displayed and stored. When necessary, preservation also encompasses the stabilization of the materials used in the creation of animation art.

With this information as a foundation, consider the following general guidelines for the preservation of animation art:

General Care

Painted Cels

A. Wear white cotton gloves when handling cels to keep them free from oils and grease, and handle cels only by their edges. Never bend or roll cels, as this could cause the character outline and colors to crack and flake off.

B. Because many of the colors used in the creation of animation cels (until recently) are water soluble, water should not come in contact with the painted areas of a cel. If it is necessary to remove dust, surface dirt, and fingerprints from a cel, use a soft, dry cotton cloth. When working this cloth horizontally over the cel, apply only a minimum amount of pressure while avoiding direct contact with the character outline and/or painted colors. Never use compressed air to clean a cel, as the character outline and colors can be easily blown away.

C. Many of the older nitrate cels are still relatively stable; however, because cellulose nitrate is a combustible material, cels of this type should be removed from their framing or storage environment once a year to air out for a period of 24–48 hours.

Story Sketches, Concept Drawings, Animation Drawings, Backgrounds
Animation art in these categories is executed with a wide variety of materials on either animation paper, colored construction paper, watercolor paper, or illustration board.

A. Animation art on paper should be handled only when necessary. Always wash hands first and handle the artwork by the edges if possible.

B. If it is handled, framed, and/or stored properly, there is no need to use a fixative for animation artwork on paper. The fixative may eventually discolor and cause as well the uneven aging of the paper itself. For pastel concept drawings, the use of a fixative unevenly saturates many of the pastel particles and should be avoided.

Framing and Display

A. To increase the longevity of animation art, use only acid-free, buffered mat board and make sure that only acid-free materials come in contact with the artwork.

B. For the most part, animation art should be framed behind a piece of ultraviolet-filtering Plexiglas®. This will minimize the damaging effects of exposure to ultraviolet light. However, because static electricity from Plexiglas can cause pastel particles to separate from its paper, pastel concept drawings should be framed behind a piece of ultraviolet-filtering glass. If possible breakage of the glass is a concern, use a piece of laminated ultraviolet-filtering glass.

C. Avoid hanging framed artwork on exterior walls, close to heating vents and fireplaces, and in or near kitchens and bathrooms, as the temperature and relative humidity fluctuate too rapidly in these areas. Even with an ultraviolet-filtering system in the framing, most animation art will still fade over time if it is displayed under a direct source of intense light. Framed artwork should therefore be displayed in areas that have a relatively stable environment and indirect, low lighting. A temperature of 68–72 degrees Fahrenheit and relative humidity of 50–55 percent represent the best possible climate ranges for animation art, while the most ideal location for display is on an interior wall that is subject to low, indirect, diffuse lighting.

D. Check the condition of framed animation art displayed in the home every three months. While slight curling in the painted cel sheet is normal, monitor any changes in the color and transparency of the cel, as well as changes in the character outline and colors. With animation art on paper, very slight undulations in the paper (especially with story sketches and animation drawings) are to be expected in many home environments; however, watch for changes in the tone and color of the paper and in the artist's materials used on it. Take a quality photograph and/or color slide of each work of art prior to display to help in detecting any changes.

Storage

A. When not on display, framed artwork should be stored vertically. Place cardboard covers over the corners of the frames or larger pieces of cardboard between framed artwork for protection.

B. Unframed animation art should only be stored flat. Avoid using polyester (such as Mylar® or Mellinex®) or acetate sheets directly against water-based painted cels and all animation art on paper. If the environmental conditions get too humid, the paint on the cel can stick to the polyester sheet or acetate. With artwork on paper, the static electricity generated from the polyester sheet or acetate can cause graphite and pastel particles to separate from the paper support over time. Given the same environmental recommendations as for animation art that is displayed, place each piece of unframed art (this applies to cels and works on paper) between its own larger folded leaf of acid-free glassine for protection during long-term storage. Then place this artwork in acid-free Solander boxes or in a similar box constructed from acid-free cardboard and acid-free tape; acid-free materials provide the most stable storage container for the artwork. Because of the fragility of the painted cels, store only one to five cels of similar size on top of one another. Ten to twenty drawings of the same size can be safely placed on top of one another.

If a work of animation art requires conservation treatment, seek an approach that combines art and science and integrates the related activities of examination and conservative restoration.

Examination

Careful viewing of animation art with the naked eye is the first step in determining its structure and the extent of any deterioration, loss, or alteration. The use of scientific, photographic, and mechanical instrumentation is an integral part of further examination, as is research into the historical background of the work of art. The information gathered to this point should be compiled in a written report and the current condition of the artwork documented photographically for future comparison should changes occur.

Conservative Restoration

Conservation treatment should stabilize the animation art and return the deteriorated or damaged work to a condition close to a form indicative of its current age. Any restoration should be confined to reintegrating the overall character design via the controlled inpainting of only those immediate areas of loss or damage. Most importantly, this should be accomplished in a manner that keeps the aesthetic and historic integrity of the artwork unchanged. Any materials used in the treatment should be tested for permanence, reliability, and (as far as practicable) their easy reversibility. Furthermore, all treatment procedures and materials should be documented with a written report and photographs. Keep this permanent record with the artwork at all times, as it facilitates monitoring the work's condition and provides for easier and safer treatment should it be necessary in the future.[24]

These guidelines outline only a few factors that are important to the care and handling of animation art. In the event of damage to or severe change in any type of animation art, contact only an experienced conservator knowledgeable about the materials and appropriate environments for this type of art, and confine the treatment to the areas of damage only. Keep in mind that the best advice is "**Less is best!**" Before any conservation treatment, document the condition of the artwork in both written and photographic form.

The Animation Process

1. Ken O'Connor, interview with the author, February 24, 1994. Prior to becoming a layout artist for *Snow White*, O'Connor drew many of the rotoscope tracings for the Snow White character.

2. William Sellers, product manager for Hammermill Premium Papers, interview with the author, January 6, 1994.

3. Although red color pencil was most common for the underdrawing, some animators preferred graphite, blue, or an ochre color pencil.

4. Frank Thomas, animator, interview with the author, February 20, 1994.

5. Betty Kimball, painter in charge of color model cels, interview with the author, February 22, 1994.

6. "Walt Disney's *Snow White and the Seven Dwarfs*," *Showplace, The Magazine of Radio City Music Hall* 2:3 (January 20, 1938):11. The actual number of cel layers used in *Snow White* may never be known. The number given here must have been based on an average of two cel layers per 1/24 of a second for the eighty-three minutes of running time of the film.

7. "Inter-Office Communication," October 15, 1928, Walt Disney Productions, Ltd.

8. Training session on inking character cels with Janet Scagnelli, owner, Chelsea Animation, Richmond, Virginia, September 8–12, 1993.

9. Notes on the typed sheets "Introduction to Painting" and "Advanced Painting." These handouts were probably prepared at the Disney studios in the late 1930s and given to the painters.

10. Sometimes very small areas of black were first applied on top (to the inked side of the cel) throughout.

11. Notes on "Introduction to Painting" and "Advanced Painting."

12. Betty Kimball interview.

13. Maurice Noble, background artist, interview with the author, February 21, 1994.

14. Ibid.

15. Shamus Culhane, *Animation from Script to Screen* (New York: St. Martin's Press, 1988), p. 247.

16. Maurice Noble interview.

17. When photographing a scene for *Snow White* with the multiplane camera, any overlays as part of the background were often painted on separate levels of glass instead of paper.

18. Maurice Noble interview.

19. Frank Thomas and Ollie Johnston, *Disney Animation: The Illusion of Life* (New York: Abbeville Press, 1981), p. 317.

Preparation of Animation Art for Sale

20. According to Betty Kimball, cels from *Snow White* were washed and then often used as blank cels that were placed between each of the painted cels, as protection, until the completed cels for a scene were photographed.

21. Cecil Munsey, *Disneyana: Walt Disney Collectibles* (New York: Hawthorn Books, Inc., 1974), p. 189.

22. Ibid.

23. Ibid., p. 190.

Conservation of Animation Art

24. For additional information on conservation approaches for works of art, see "Code of Ethics and Standards of Practice," American Institute for the Conservation of Historic and Artistic Works (AIC), 1717 K Street, N.W., Suite 301, Washington, D.C., 20006.

Glossary

animation:
the process of creating motion from frame-by-frame techniques in filmmaking. In cel animation, the animated characters are first drawn on paper and then traced and painted onto cels. The painted cels are then placed over a background and photographed one frame at a time. When the completed film is projected at a rate of twenty-four frames per second, the illusion of motion is created.

animator:
an artist who, in rough form, creates the extreme drawings of the character action for a scene.

assistant animator:
an artist who cleans up the animator's rough drawings. At times the assistant animator may also draw some of the inbetweens for a scene, leaving any remaining drawings for the inbetweener.

background:
a finished rendering from the final layout drawing that provides the setting for the character action and, if necessary, special effects.

cel level:
the order and number of levels (A–D and, in extreme cases, E), initially indicated on the animation drawings, in which the character cel and/or special effect cels are to occur per frame of action. In some instances different portions of a character's action are broken down into different levels.

cel setup:
a setup that consists of the production background, on top of which one to four layers of cels are registered, and that constitutes the elements of a scene as it would be seen in one frame of film.

cel:
shortened term for celluloid. See "celluloid."

celluloid:
a thin sheet of clear cellulose nitrate (or, since the early 1940s, cellulose acetate) on which the character or special effects are painted. The painted cels are then placed over the background as they would occur per frame of film and photographed one frame at a time. Several cels are therefore photographed sequentially over one production background.

character color:
the specific range of colors for a character that are painted onto the back of the cel.

character outline:
the linear line on the front of the cel denoting the forms and shapes of the character.

checker:
the person who checks all the completed elements of a scene against the notations on the corresponding exposure sheet to ensure that everything is correct for the camera.

clean-up / clean-up animation:
the process of converting the rough, sketchy animation drawings into smooth, clean lines by retracing each animation rough onto a new piece of animation paper.

color model cel:
painted character cel that shows the colors for a given character. The color model cel is used as an aid in finalizing the character colors for a scene and determining the colors for the production background of that scene.

color model drawing:
linear drawing of a character on animation paper in which the specific colors for that character are indicated.

color separation lines:
lines initially made on the clean-up animation drawings with different color pencils to indicate areas in which a different color ink line is to be used by the inker when he or she traces the outline of a character onto the front of the cel.

color study:
see "preliminary background."

dailies:
the filmed portion of a scene that is processed the previous night by the laboratory.

director:
the person in charge of the various production stages of a feature.

drawing level:
see "cel level."

drawing numbers:
the sequential numbering of each animation drawing for a scene. These numbers correspond to the numbers written for each frame of film on the exposure sheet for that scene.

exposure sheet:
a form in which the dialogue, character, and special effects action, cel number and level, as well as notations for the camera are indicated per frame of film for a given scene.

extremes:
animation drawings indicating the extreme points of character action.

field line:
a rough linear line along the sides, top, or bottom of the cel that indicates the parameters for the colors of a character. This line is applied to the front of the cel when the inker traces the character outline from the clean-up drawing.

field:
the area of a scene that will be in view when photographed by the camera.

final layout:
see "layout."

inbetweener:
an artist who creates the drawings that occur between the animator's extremes and any other drawings done by the assistant animator.

inbetweens:
animation drawings indicating the character action as it occurs between the extremes.

inker:
the person who traces the outline from the clean-up drawing onto the front of the cel with ink.

inking:
the process of tracing with ink or thinned paint the character outline, object, or special effect onto the front of the cel by hand.

key setup:
see "cel setup."

layout:
a drawing showing the scale, perspective, and elements of a background. The size of the characters and their path of action are also indicated on the layout. Initially the layout is drawn in rough form. Once the character action has been okayed for clean up, a final layout is created in accurate detail.

let-down:
a calculated darker and grayer color value that, when painted onto a cel, compensates for the graying and increased density of each cel level created when one to four cels are placed on top of one another per frame of film.

mask cel:
a cel in which a portion is painted with black paint—with either a brush or airbrush. The mask cel is placed over the portion of a background or character that is in shadow and photographed with the corresponding cels and backgrounds at a portion of the total time necessary for that scene.

master background:
see " production background."

model sheet:
a sheet of paper on which several different views of a character are illustrated. The model sheet serves as a guide for the animator and assistants to the appearance and construction of a character.

moviola:
a projection machine used by the animators to view pencil tests.

overlay:
separate areas in the foreground of a scene behind which portions of the character action occur. An overlay may be painted onto a separate piece of paper, glass, or cel.

painter:
the person who paints colors onto the back of the cel.

painting:
the process of applying the character colors onto the back of the cel by hand.

pan:
the process in which the camera appears to move horizontally or vertically across a scene. This sense of movement is accomplished by moving the elements of a scene in one direction under the camera.

peg bar:
a metal (or, more recently, plastic) bar with a series of small pegs. All the animation paper, cels, and background art are punched with holes that correspond to the peg system, which supports the artwork and keeps it in registration throughout the stages of production.

pencil test:
the process of photographing frame by frame the rough and clean-up animation drawings for a scene in order to critique the pencil animation for smoothness when the film is projected. To save printing time and expenses, the pencil tests are viewed in their negative form— white pencil lines against a black background.

preliminary background:
moderately rendered backgrounds that are painted with the selected colors for a scene as a color study for the production background.

production background:
a painted background used in the production of an animated film. Also, see "background."

rotoscope:
a machine that projects live-action film footage onto a drawing table one frame at a time so that the image can be traced onto animation paper. The resulting rotoscope tracings served as guides from which the animator created lifelike movement.

rough layout:
see "layout."

roughs / rough animation:
the process of creating a series of rough, sketchy drawings that indicate the character action for a scene.

scene:
a portion of a film that depicts one situation.

self-ink lines / self-lines:
see "color separation lines."

sequence:
a series of related scenes that, combined, depict a portion of the story.

soundtrack:
that portion of a film comprised of voices, music, and sound effects.

spacing chart:
a simple graphlike diagram made by the animator, usually in the bottom right corner of the drawing, to indicate the number and spacing of drawings that are to occur between the extremes.

story reel:
the timed, filmed version of the story sketches in order, enabling the director to have an early understanding of the sequence and total length of the animated feature.

story sketch:
a sketch, often drawn on animation paper, that depicts a portion of a story.

storyboard:
a large cork board to which story sketches are pinned in comic strip fashion in an order that tells the complete story.

sweatbox:
a small room in which portions of a film are viewed for critique.

synchronization:
when the sound and picture elements of a film are occurring in unison.

thumbnail sketch:
a very rough drawing that is one to three inches in size.

trace-backs:
the portion of a figure that does not move on the screen and is traced from a previous drawing onto one or more consecutive cels by the inker.

truck:
the process in which the camera moves toward or away from the elements of a scene.

working reel:
a working copy of the film, begun by photographing the story sketches on the storyboard for each scene. These scenes are spliced together in their proper order to illustrate the film in rough form from beginning to end. As a scene is completed in rough animation, it is filmed and put into the working reel in place of the corresponding filmed story sketches. This replacement process continues with each scene through rough and clean-up animation, as well as with the painted cels and backgrounds, until the entire film is completed in color.

Bibliography

Articles

Allan, Robin. "The fairest film of all: *Snow White* reassessed." *Animator* 21 (October–December 1987):18–21.

American Institute for Conservation of Historic and Artistic Works (AIC). "Code of Ethics and Standards of Practice." *1994 Directory, the American Institute for Conservation of Historic and Artistic Works* (1993):21–34.

Caselotti, Adriana, and Brian Sibley. "With a smile and a song." *Animator* 21 (October–December 1987):22–23.

Disney, Walt. "Snow White." *Showplace, The Magazine of Radio City Music Hall* 2:3 (January 20, 1938):7–14.

Grafly, Dorothy. "America's Youngest Art." *The American Magazine of Art* 26:7 (July 1933):336–42.

Green, Howard. "Epics of Animation: *Snow White and the Seven Dwarfs.*" *Cinemagic* 36 (1987):40–45, 66–67.

Hulett, Ralph. "The Artist's Part in the Production of an Animated Cartoon." *American Artist* 19:5 (May 1955):31 ff.

Stillwell, Miriam. "The Story Behind Snow White's $10,000,000 Surprise Party." *Liberty* (April 9, 1938):7–8.

Books

Abrams, Robert E. (preface), and John Canemaker (introduction). *Treasures of Disney Animation Art.* New York: Abbeville Press, 1982.

Culhane, Shamus. *Animation from Script to Screen.* New York: St. Martin's Press, 1988.

Doerner, Max. *The Materials of the Artist and Their Use in Painting.* Rev. ed. New York: Harcourt, Brace and Co., 1949.

Feild, Robert D. *The Art of Walt Disney.* New York: The Macmillan Company, 1942.

Finch, Christopher. *The Art of Walt Disney.* New York: Abrams, 1973.

Grant, John. *Encyclopedia of Walt Disney's Animated Characters.* New York: Hyperion, 1993.

Holliss, Richard, and Brian Sibley. *Walt Disney's Snow White and the Seven Dwarfs & the Making of the Classic Film.* New York: Simon & Schuster, Inc., 1987.

Hunter, Dard. *Papermaking: The History and Technique of an Ancient Craft.* New York: Dover Publications, Inc., 1974.

Los Angeles County Museum. *Retrospective Exhibition of the Walt Disney Medium.* 1940.

Maltin, Leonard. *Of Mice and Magic.* New York: McGraw-Hill Book Company, 1980.

Mayer, Ralph. *The Artist's Handbook of Materials and Techniques.* Third ed. New York: The Viking Press, 1970.

Munsey, Cecil. *Disneyana: Walt Disney Collectibles.* New York: Hawthorn Books, Inc., 1974.

Solomon, Charles. *Enchanted Drawings—The History of Animation.* New York: Alfred A. Knopf, 1989.

Thomas, Bob. *The Art of Animation.* Jamestown, Ohio: Golden Press, 1958.

——*Disney's Art of Animation: From Mickey Mouse to Beauty and the Beast.* New York: Hyperion, 1991.

——*Walt Disney: An American Original.* New York: Simon and Schuster, 1976.

Thomas, Frank, and Ollie Johnston. *Disney Animation: The Illusion of Life.* New York: Abbeville Press, 1981.

Wehlte, Kurt. *The Materials and Techniques of Painting.* New York: Van Nostrand Reinhold Co., 1982.

Acknowledgments

When he committed *Snow White and the Seven Dwarfs* to film in 1937, Walt Disney believed—though he could not be certain—that the world was ready for a feature-length animated motion picture. Happily, *Snow White* found its audience. Those involved in the preparation of this book and the exhibition it accompanies launch their more modest enterprise in the same spirit and with the same high hopes for a successful outcome.

The film and this book about its creation are kindred collaborative enterprises in yet another way: Both demanded the melding of many individual talents into a cohesive whole. It is my pleasant task to acknowledge the contributions of those whose talents have been so melded.

I first want to thank those original members of Disney's creative team who generously shared their recollections with our authors, thus allowing us to revisit in imagination Disney's Hyperion Avenue studio during those pivotal years 1934 to 1937: Frank Thomas, Ollie Johnston, Marc Davis, Joe Grant, Ken O'Connor, Maurice Noble, Harry Tytle, Jack Hannah, and Ward and Betty Kimball. All were involved in the creation of the thousands of individual images that through the magic of animation were transformed into a single work of art.

Steve Ison has made it his crusade for the last decade to collect and preserve these fragile components of a uniquely American art form. The obvious pleasure he takes in his quest has energized us all. In bringing the same level of commitment and enthusiasm to this project, he has become more than a lender—he has been our partner.

Steve would particularly like to thank his wife, Nancy, his "fairest one of all," for suggesting years ago that he "get a hobby" and for her understanding once he found one. He thanks his children, Nicholas and Brittany, for providing him inspiration, purpose, and unquestioned forgiveness each time he neglected their quality time together when he was off on his crusade. He would like to acknowledge the contributions of his assistant, Sue Postlewaite, "Listener of Complaints and Opinions, Tracker of Lost Art, and Organizer of Cryptic Notes." He would like to thank his fellow collectors Mike Glad, Peter Merolo, John Snyder, and Jeff Lotman, who share his passion, and for providing the agony of defeat and the thrill of victory throughout the many years of mutual quests for animation treasures.

Martin Krause, our curator of prints, drawings, and photographs, has been the animating spirit, so to speak, of this creative enterprise. So wholeheartedly has he thrown himself into the process (whistling cheerfully all the while) that he might almost have been taken for a latter-day recruit to the original septet, in which company his physical stature surely would have earned him the soubriquet "Lanky." Martin has written the lead essay and overseen every aspect of the exhibition's organization with his customary thoroughness, imagination, and creativity.

Linda Witkowski, our associate conservator of paintings, has written a treatise on animation and a unique guide to the care and handling of animation art that is both thoroughly researched and eminently readable. Her love of animation art is both professional and personal. She wishes to thank her colleagues David Miller, Monica Radecki, and Neil Cockerline, who served her as sounding boards.

The photographic talents of John Geiser are evident on every page of this book. He photographed each work, many of them for the first time since 1937, when they were on the animation camera stand at Walt Disney Studios. He would like to remember the assistance of Ruth Roberts. Jane Graham, publications manager, has steered this book to completion with her customary attention to detail and with her broad intelligence.

Ellen Lee, senior curator; Martin Radecki, chief conservator; and Mary Bergerson, director of marketing, have been ever supportive of this novel project. Meg Gammage-Tucker and Susan Albers have taken in hand the search for support of a more practical nature. Karin Frick and Suellen Mazzuca deciphered the manuscripts into typescripts, which have been edited with customary precision and sensitivity by Debra Edelstein. The design and production of a classic book on a classic film was the responsibility of J. Michael Hayes and Megan Umbanhowar of JMH Corporation.

Our project would never have succeeded without the encouragement of those at The Walt Disney Company who freely provided guidance and information. We appreciate the interest of Roy E. Disney and the assistance of Wayne Smith and David Kopp at Disney Art Editions and Dave Pacheco of Disney Publications. David Smith and Robert Tieman of the Walt Disney Archives and Kay Salz of the Disney Animation Research Library reviewed the texts for accuracy. William Sellers of Hammermill Premium Papers and Janet Scagnelli of Chelsea Animation provided valuable pieces of technical information. We particularly appreciate the efforts of those at Hyperion, notably publisher Robert Miller and Lesley Krauss, who have forged a partnership with us in this publication.

The exhibition required other efforts and talents: Angela Berg, print room manager; Sherman O'Hara, exhibits designer; Vanessa Wicker Burkhart and her team of registrars; Mona Slaton and her corps of marketing specialists; Brian Hogarth and his fellow museum educators, and virtually every other member of the museum staff, all of whom deserve my thanks for their efforts on this project.

Walt Disney was faced with the similarly impossible task of expressing his appreciation to the more than 750 artists, technicians, musicians, and writers who contributed to the four-year genesis of *Snow White and the Seven Dwarfs*. I can do no better than to echo the words with which Disney opened the movie's credits: "My sincere appreciation to the members of my staff whose loyalty and creative endeavor made possible this production."

Bret Waller
Director
Indianapolis Museum of Art

Index